# STUDIES IN AFRICAN AMERICAN HISTORY AND CULTURE

*Edited by*
## Graham Hodges
Colgate University

## A ROUTLEDGE SERIES

# STUDIES IN AFRICAN AMERICAN HISTORY AND CULTURE

GRAHAM HODGES, *General Editor*

# BOYS, BOYZ, BOIS
## An Ethics of Black Masculinity in
## Film and Popular Media

Keith M. Harris

Routledge
New York & London

An earlier version of chapter 5 was published as Harris, Keith M. "'Untitled': D'Angelo and the Visualization of the Black Male Body." *Wide Angle*, Volume 21, Number 4 (October 1999), 62-83. Reprinted courtesy of *Wide Angle* and Johns Hopkins University Press.

Published in 2006 by
Routledge
Taylor & Francis Group
270 Madison Avenue
New York, NY 10016

Published in Great Britain by
Routledge
Taylor & Francis Group
2 Park Square
Milton Park, Abingdon
Oxon OX14 4RN

Printed in the United States of America on acid-free paper
10 9 8 7 6 5 4 3 2 1

International Standard Book Number-10: 0-415-97578-6 (Hardcover)
International Standard Book Number-13: 978-0-415-97578-0 (Hardcover)
Library of Congress Card Number 2005025830

### Library of Congress Cataloging-in-Publication Data

Harris, Keith M.
   Boys, boyz, bois : an ethics of Black masculinity in film and popular media / Keith M. Harris.
      p. cm. -- (Studies in African American history and culture)
   Includes bibliographical references and index.
   ISBN 0-415-97578-6
   1. African American men in motion pictures. 2. African American men in popular culture. 3. Masculinity in motion pictures. 4. Masculinity in popular culture. I. Title. II. Series.

PN1995.9.N4H37 2006
791.43'652108996073--dc22                                    2005025830

Visit the Taylor & Francis Web site at
http://www.taylorandfrancis.com

Taylor & Francis Group
is the Academic Division of Informa plc.

and the Routledge Web site at
http://www.routledge-ny.com

*This book is dedicated to the memory of Mrs. Sophia L. S. Hart,
Dr. Barbara Christian, and Dr. Bill Nestrick*

# Contents

# Preface

*Boys, Boyz, Bois* is the synthesis and culmination of research and writing about cinema and black masculinity. My critical interrogation of cinema and black masculinity began in graduate school in the 1980s and 90s. Consequently, much of the theorizing on race and masculinity springs from the then popular social and media construct of the black man as "endangered species" and with the black cinema renaissance ushered in by Spike Lee and others in the mid-80s. As a consequence, the objects of study are largely representative of that period. Since the beginning of my research, a lot has been written about black masculinity in particular. The project of this book is, on the one hand, an evaluation and critique of some of this writing, especially the writing emerging from the fields of cultural studies, cinema studies, and gender studies. On the other hand, this book is an insertion into the existing debates about black masculinity. From this standpoint, I raise the question of ethics and gender and race. By shifting the question away from the social construction to the ethical construction of race and gender, this book constitutes a critique and an evaluation not only of masculinity, but also of traditional notions of ethics.

However, this book is not a philosophical treatise on ethics. Instead, ethics and ethical questions provide the ground for site specific examinations of theories, texts and personae. Chapter One provides a theoretical and historical context for examining black masculinity and black cinema. This chapter provides the frameworks for defining masculinity in relation to film, media and racial performativity. Also, this chapter provides working definitions and periodizations of "black cinema" through Lott (1991) and Yearwood (2000). Furthermore, the notion of racial performativity and the delineations of black cinema provide critical lines of thought which run throughout the book. Following Chapter One, there are four specific sites of analysis: 1). Sidney Poitier and filmic black masculinity; 2). Blaxploitation and the authenticity of black masculinity; 3). New Black Cinema and the hermeneutic shift to Post-New Black Cinema; and 4). the visualization of blackness, the black body and masculinity in visual culture and music video.

Chapters Two and Three situate my project and contemporary debates about black masculinity in relation to Blaxploitation films. The argument is that Blaxploitation marks a significant change in the encoding of blackness, marking a turning point in the representation of African Americans, specifically African American men, in film. As such, I argue that Blaxploitation films are not black cinema as it has recently been defined and that Blaxploitation films, as exploitation films, perform an exaltation of symbolic blackness, which serves to mask historical blackness. On the one hand, there is the conflicting counter argument, which I make as well, that these films are about African Americans in that they are targeted and marketed specifically to African Americans, drawing on then contemporary debates about blackness, black power, and current social concerns of crime and community. As representations of African Americans in preceding eras of American film, however, the figures of black masculinity in Blaxploitation films, though continuous as stereotypical depictions, are markedly different articulations of blackness, sexuality, and cultural and social agency. Therefore, in elaboration of the difference, Chapter Two includes an extended discussion of Sidney Poitier as a celebrity and figure of black masculinity from which the Blaxploitation figures of masculinity articulate difference and opposition. This chapter proceeds from discussions of Poitier's films and his autobiographical work in *This Life* (1980) and is followed in Chapter Three by definitions of exploitation and Blaxploitation films. This requires that Chapter Three offer some explication of exploitation films as a kind of film with specific formal aspects that separate them and define them apart from and against "quality" productions. Chapter Three concludes with a discussion of how the notions of black masculinity, as pre-figured in Blaxploitation and the then contemporary debates surrounding these films, guide the discussion of masculinity in the following period of production, New Black Cinema.

The fourth chapter examines film practices and situates the notions of masculinity which emerged in New Black Cinema. The approach to this material is through textual analysis and film history. My argument is that black filmmakers necessarily have to deal especially with two moments in American film history, the period of *Birth of a Nation* and the period of Blaxploitation films. These films offer a corrective re-coding of the representations of blacks in film. With the more recent films, notions of masculinity are steeped in the rhetoric of nation and discourse of nationalism, which propose masculine formations as signs of community and self-determination. This chapter concludes with a discussion of Post-New Black Cinema, another periodization in which, I argue, there has been a shift in blackness as a signifier which, in turn, produces blackness as a more encompassing critical hermeneutic device in popular black cultural productions.

In Chapter Five, I introduce the category of *bois* through the examination of the music video, "How does it feel," and the soul persona of D'Angelo. My intention is to interrogate questions of form and textuality in the video and to examine ways in which the form of the music video, and this video in particular, raise questions of spectatorship. I argue that the video, its intertextual dialog with visual culture (photography specifically), and the contemporary hip-hop black masculine engender certain critical responses which engage the spectator in ethical questions about masculinity and about the contemporary black masculinity.

This book has been a long process and I am indebted to so many people. I would like to thank Manthia Diawara, Ed Guerrero, Josè Munoz and, especially, Toby Miller, whose guidance and commitment to my project has been a source of immeasurable support. I would like to extend my gratitude to the New York University community at large, but especially to the following: Mia, Alondra, Donette, Sam, Alessandra, Michael, Lorca, Stewart, and the Department of Cinema Studies. Also I would like to thank the extended University of California at Berkeley and San Diego communities: Frederick, Randy, Andy, Helen, Donna and Rakesh, Carolina, Alberto, and especially Ricardo (the reader supreme) and the late Drs. Barbara Christian and Bill Nestrick. The New York City Group, I owe you a lot: Charles, Danny, Norman, Victor, Antonio and Frederique and the Noodle Pudding Crew, and Bruno and Nino. To the friends and supporters at Ohio University, I would like to thank the following: The Schools of Interdisciplinary Arts and Film, the Department of African American Studies, and Maura, Bradley, and Mr. Butler. And finally, I would like to thank my mother, Mrs. Ruth S. H. Harris, and my family, for the years of support. And a special thanks to my sister, Tonya, without whom none of this would have come to past.

# Introduction

The play on the word *boy* in the main title, *Boys, Boyz, Bois,* has various functions: First, as a point of reference, the use of *boy* signifies that this is part of an ongoing project in contemporary discussions and debates about gender and masculinity. Second, the use of the plural forms (*-s, -z, -is*) refers to the desire to discuss multiples in reference to a singular idea—if not monolithic category. Third, a second point about multiples, the multiple spellings signify not only more than one of the same (more than one boy or plurality), but also more than one, which is different from the same (more than one kind of boy or variety). In other words, the multiples of the same refer to an exchange between sameness and difference in signification. Fourth, the use of the standard plural *boys,* with the *–s,* specifically refers to an ideal form of boy, an idealization of masculinity which is fixed, traditionally positing gender as natural and biological. Furthermore, in a racially and ethnically stratified society, this idealized *boy* is simultaneously a racial and ethnic idealization of whiteness (and masculinity) and a racist denigration, an infantilization of blackness (and racialized masculinity). Fifth, in opposition to *boys, boyz* refers to the currently popular spelling of, and popular contemporary figure of, the black masculine in hip-hop and popular culture. *Boyz* is, on the one hand, a re-articulation of *boys* within the discourse of racialized masculinity, in which the notion of black masculinity is given privilege as a signifier of masculinity; on the other hand, as a contemporary signifier of the black masculine, *boyz* is a signifier of youth and an age/ethos of urban blackness. And sixth, an opposition to *boys* and *boyz,* the use of *bois* signifies an *other* form of masculinity. *Bois,* a heuristic *boy,* is a construct which functions as a variation or that poses itself as an alternative. It is these three "boys" that I have put in conversation in order to develop the project, *The ethics of black masculinity in film and popular media.*

1

The contemplation of ethics as an ethics of gender, and specifically as an ethics of masculinity, is a difficult task, indeed. I have, however, chosen this path in order to illuminate not only questions of gender, but also questions of race. With race and gender intersecting and overlapping in social interactions and subjective formations, it becomes clearer that gender and race provide frameworks for perception, understanding, imagining, and aestheticizing. Gender and race constitute, as various modes of perception and understanding, a form of knowledge. Furthermore, notions of gender and race provide ways of performing actions, ways of doing things, and the concepts of gender and race (as "actions" of aesthetics) function in the praxis and performance of gender and race. It is in this nexus of gender and race as knowledge and actions/performance at which I raise questions of ethics as questions of the uses of gender and race and the problems that arise when considering gender and race in this manner.[1]

Therefore, the project here is an interrogation of notions of masculinity, black masculinity, and masculinities in general as they articulate, negotiate, and contend as discursive subject formations in public discourse and in popular media. In doing so, I explore black public figures in their given media as discursive subjects involved in performative and critical practice, through cultural production. In order to do this, I examine masculinity through questions of ethics, through an ethics of masculinity. By positing public figures as critics in critical praxis and emphasizing notions of gender and race within performativity, the project becomes an evaluation of the efficacy of a given gender and racial performative figure within ethics and the conduct and care of the self.

## RACE AND ETHICAL DISCOURSE

I am using two notions of ethics. First, ethics refers to the more philosophical notion in which ethics is the study of the nature of morals and of specific morals choices. It is with this idea of ethics that I examine concepts of the good life, codes of conduct, and systems of moral valuation. Ethics as a philosophical study of morality is much debated and contested. It is not my intention to enter into any debate or contestation of ethics as a philosophical discourse. Instead, I am interested in the stable concepts of ethics, the concepts of the "good life," "goodness," moral conduct and responsibility, and notions of happiness and the pursuit of happiness. I am interested in how these concepts are formed and shaped by and alongside categories of race and gender.

Therefore, part of this project is informed by the work of Charles W. Mills (1997 and 1998), in which racial discourses and their critiques are used to examine philosophical categories and concepts. Drawing on the

Kantian concept of the ideal person, Mills disengages conceptual and theoretical notions of race embedded in the seemingly universal "ideal person"
and personhood in Kant's ethical and moral discourses. I have chosen Kant
as the primary text for the philosophical investigation of race, gender, and
ethics because, in agreement with Mills, Kant's moral and political investigations are "the best articulation of the moral egalitarianism associated
with the Enlightenment, the American and French revolutions" (Mills
1998, 68). As such Kant is situated in contemporary debates about race
and the Enlightenment and the incompletion and/or failure of the Enlightenment (our "we are not yet modern" debate), especially since these
debates are also integral to critical race theory, African American studies,
and gender studies (see Gilroy 1993; Habermas 1983; and Lott 1999).
Also, the concepts of personhood and respect, which are central to Kant's
moral theory, provide an intimate site for the exchange and dialog between
African American discourse and discursive engagement with those very
concepts, *viz.* the ideas of manhood and respect.

Using contractarian theory, Mills argues that the social contract
underlying Kant's ethical theory is also, in light of actual practice, an
instantiation of the Racial Contract:

> The 'Racial Contract' I employ is in a sense more in keeping with the
> spirit of the classic contractarians—Hobbes, Locke, Rousseau, and Kant.
> I use it not merely normatively, to generate judgments about social justice
> and injustice, but descriptively, to *explain* the actual genesis of the society
> and the state, the way society is structured, the way the government func-
> tions, and people's moral psychology (Mills 1997, 5).

The Racial Contract provides a concept through which the traditional
social contract is re-conceptualized within the cultural logic of imperialism
and colonialism and as a set of disciplinary practices and theory of society
in which questions of race and domination are brought to task as non-ide-
alized/naturalized practices of an ideal social contract (4–6).

For Kant, the social contract is one of rationality and respect between
ideal persons and allows for the development of traditional notions of
moral obligations, the development of "what one ought to do" (Kymlicka
1991, 191). The Kantian ideal person exists in a formal, abstracted moral
universe in which "persons" are rational, self-controlling, conscience bearing individuals. Persons are morally bound by the commands of duty to
other persons and community (Kant 1797 and 1785). There is a clear
demarcation between the moral status of persons and non-persons, those
with moral standing and agency and those without, respectively:

In the system of nature, a human (*homo phaenomenon, animal rationale*) is a being of slight importance and shares with the rest of the animals, as offspring of the earth, an ordinary value. Although a human being has, in his understanding, something more than they and can set himself ends, even this gives him only an *extrinsic* value for his usefulness; that is to say, it gives one man a higher value than another, that is a *price* as a commodity in exchange with these animals as things, though he still has a lower value than the universal medium of exchange, money, the value of which can therefore be called preeminent.

But a human being regarded as a *person,* that is, as the subject of morally practical reason, is exalted above any price; for as a person (*homo noumenon*) he is not to be valued merely as a means to the ends of others or even to his own ends, but as a end in himself, that is, he possesses a *dignity* (an absolute inner worth) by which he exacts *respect* for himself from all other rational beings in the world. He can measure himself with every other being of this kind and value himself on a footing of equality with them.

Humanity in his person is the object of respect which he can demand from every other human, but which he must also not forfeit. Hence he can and should value himself by a low as well as by a high standard, depending on whether he views himself as a sensible being. . . . Since he must regard himself not only as a person generally but also as a *human being,* that is, as a person who has duties his own reason lays upon him, his insignificance as a *human animal* may not infringe upon his consciousness of his dignity as a *rational human being,* . . . (*The Metaphysics of Morals* 1797, 186–187).

I have quoted Kant at length in order to demonstrate how Kant makes a distinction between phenomenal and noumenal properties and categories. The phenomenal is the empirical, the physical (*homo phaenomenon,* "the offspring of the earth"), and the noumenal is the intelligible, the moral being (*homo noumenon*). In Mills' reading, this distinction between the sensible and the intelligible is what is rendered as sub-person and person, respectively, when situated within Kant's anthropology of man. On the one hand, "race" in a Kantian schema is a phenomenal difference; on the other hand, as "race" (and categories and groupings of man) appears in Kant's anthropology, it is a contradictory idea, one which cannot allow an ascent, *viz.* reason, dignity and respect, to the noumenal man.

Furthermore, upon a closer examination of Kant's anthropology, the phenomenal and noumenal are also temporally and spatially inflected.[2] The transformation of phenomenal man to the noumenal man, from the senses to reason, is a temporal and spatial move, which in the discourse of morality is a form of subjectification, a move from the object of morality to the subject of morality. Temporally, the phenomenal non-person (Mills' "sub-person") lacks, or is denied, coevalness. By coevalness, and the lack of it, I am suggesting that there is a physical and epistemological distancing within temporal relations between noumenal persons and phenomenal non-persons. It is the denial of coevalness which renders the phenomenal non-persons object of paternal authority.[3] Spatially, the non-person occupies the temporal space of savagery versus the person's space of culture and civilization.

Mills suggests that within traditional philosophical discourse African Americans (woman and other ethnic and "racial" groups) have been denied personhood or have been theoretically conceived of as lacking personhood. This denial or lack is, for Mills, one of the defining features of the African American experience, a structuring absence which has ramifications in multiple and overlapping spheres of public and private life (Mills 1998, 6). Through an examination of this structuring absence, Mills concludes that an organizing principle in African American thought, philosophy, and cultural production becomes that of the "sub-person"[4]:

> . . . [T]he peculiar status of a subperson is that it is an entity which, because of phenotype, seems (from, of course, the perspective of the categorizer) human in some respects but not in others. It is a human . . . who, though adult, is not fully a person. And the tensions and internal contradictions in this concept capture the tensions and internal contradictions of the black experience in a white-supremacist society (Mills 1998, 6).

Mills suggests that there are different philosophical "terrains," terrains of epistemology, ethics, aesthetics, and politics that are mapped according to racial divisions of personhood and sub-personhood:

> From the beginning [of Western philosophy], therefore, the problems faced by those categorized as persons and those categorized as subpersons will be radically different. One can no longer speak with quite such assurance of *the* problems of philosophy; rather, these are problems of *particular* groups of human beings, and for others there will be different kinds of problems that are far more urgent. A relativizing of the discipline's traditional hierarchies of importance and centrality becomes necessary (10).

The first, more traditional notion of ethics employed here is informed by this "relativizing." Relativizing is, in this instance, not a post-modern perspectivalism, as much as it is a hermeneutic. In other words, the relativizing of traditional notions of philosophical concepts offers a manner in which these concepts can be held accountable (the actual vs. the ideal), not as a relativizing of meaning; furthermore, this relativizing is a form of estrangement which opens a space for interrogation and critique.[5]

Mills' relativizing is, however, in the same paradigm of racial and cultural theory that informs the concept of double consciousness (twoness, the veil, second-sight), used by DuBois to describe the particular African American racial experience (DuBois 1903a). Double consciousness, though more so in an American pragmatic tradition, provides a problematic akin to the person and the sub-person as two sightedness, as seeing across the veil, as akin to the problematic of the American and the African American, or as "an American, a Negro; two souls; two thoughts; two strivings . . ." (364). Whereas the category of sub-person is one of accountability, the concept of double consciousness theorizes a critical consciousness and praxis of racial subjects in their lived-world experience.

For the purpose of this project, the sub-person and double consciousness are used to interrogate black masculinities and what Lewis Gordon identifies as "existence in black" (Gordon 1997). "Race" and racial experience, as this experience is expressed through performative black masculinities, become the lens through which orthodox categories, notions, and concepts of ethics, value, and morality are examined. This "relativizing" becomes necessary as a way of addressing discourses of black masculinity and femininity which place race and gender in a sub-universe, a sub-universe in which black men and women are categorically morally separated through ethical valuations and social evaluations, such as images of the dysfunctional family, the endangered species (or endangered black man) and the single mother (or welfare mother), or the landscapes and mediascapes of the inner city, the black ghetto and the culture of poverty, or in the codification of social problems as racial atavism in the tropes of Willie Horton and O.J. Simpson, "wilding," "thugz," and gang warfare. It becomes necessary to discuss these various tropes of blackness and gender as they relate to ethical discourse and constructs of ethical behavior not only in their construction and perpetuation in the media, but also in their use and appropriation by cultural practitioners.

This split or bifurcated notion of person and sub-persons allows for an understanding of experience and identity as they are frequently used to comment on and deploy critique of both experience and identity themselves and ethics and politics. In other words, the concept of sub-personhood provides a site for understanding and reading alternative and perspectival discourses of race and gender proposed in contemporary cultural production, providing a framework to discuss race and gender as these two notions are understood to be "sociogenic," historicized, and structured in practice.[6] Therefore, within the relationship to philosophy and the knowledge and actions of race and gender, I argue that black masculinity is dialogic in its relationship to traditional notions of masculinity and traditional forms of knowledge posited alongside masculinity.[7] Black masculinity, then, becomes a site of contestation. Indeed, the dialogic characteristic of blackness and gender become a situation of interpretation, constructing a performative hermeneutic which is in dialog with masculinity, tradition, race, and identity, as they are all engaged in contest and debate.

At this juncture the second notion of ethics informing my project is clearer. With this second aspect, ethics refers to the care of the self as a practice of ethical subject formation. For this notion of ethics, I perform an analysis of ethico-political subjective formations, and I draw upon Foucault's idea of four "technologies" and their maintenance and governance of the self (Foucault 1988, 18). Of Foucault's technologies, "matrix[ces] of practical reason," two are important for my purpose here: 1). technologies of power; and 2). technologies of the self.[8] Technologies of power determine the conduct of individuals, fashioning and defining subjects within particular discourses. Technologies of the self are means by which individuals transform themselves into seemingly autonomous subjects in pursuit of happiness (18). My intention is to examine these two technologies and the interrelations between the two and reveal ways in which technologies of power and technologies of the self are deployed in critical strategies of pedagogy and the social figures of the critic.

In an elaboration of technologies of power and technologies of the self, I map the technologies onto the studies of Pierre Bourdieu and, in particular, his notions of *habitus* and field (Bourdieu 1993 and 1990). These constitutive categories describe ways in which social formations and texts inscribe and transform various critical and social discourses and the social conditions from which these formations and texts are then articulated in a social field. The *habitus* describes a practice, a way of being, or a "feel for the game":

> The conditionings associated with a particular call of conditions of existence produce *habitus,* systems of durable, transposable dispositions, structured structures predisposed to function as structuring structures, that is, as principles which generate and organize practices and representations that can be objectively adapted to their outcomes without presupposing a conscious aiming at ends or an express mastery of the operations necessary in order to attain them. Objectively 'regulated'

and 'regular' without being in any way the product of obedience to rules, . . . (1990, 53).

The *habitus*, then, is part of a process of socialization and inculcation, becoming a set of "second nature" dispositions. For the purpose here *habitus* provides a way of understanding race and gender as practice, as ways of being.

However, there is certain determinism in this configuration of *habitus*. In order to account for this and elaborate *habitus* as a notion of the agent with agency against determinism, Bourdieu situates *habitus* in what he calls a field, or fields. A field is a structure of objective social relations. Any social agent is structured by the organization of these fields (*e.g.*, economic, political, religious, educational fields, etc.), each of which have their own organization independent of each other. Furthermore, at any instance, the structure and operation of any given field is governed by the relationship between persons that operate in a given field. In this way, the field functions as a contextualization device, a contest or situation for the practice of *habitus* (1990, 66–68). Bourdieu likens the relationship between *habitus* and field as one between "incorporated history" (*habitus*) and "objective history" (field).

Foucault's technologies of power and technologies of the self meet in Bourdieu's notions of *habitus* and field, as it seems that it is in the field that the domination of the self and the fashioning of the self are most revealed. This overlaying of the *habitus* and field and technologies of power and technologies of the self does two things: First, it allows for the further establishment of the nexus of technologies of power and self as an intertextual network, allowing for the negotiation of the category of the field as a *process* engaged in modes and strategies of training and intellectual and self modification that are fluid and dynamic; second, this overlap allows me to form, from the technology of the self, a final product, practice, which in turn will allow for a greater examination of performative modes, normative and alternative, of gender and race as they are assumed in a given medium and represented in a given cultural production.

Important to the use of technologies of power and technologies of the self is the notion of the subject of critical analysis as one of ethical incompleteness (Hunter 1988a and 1988b; and Miller 1993). As an ethically incomplete subject, the task of criticism becomes one of inscribing indeterminancy in relation to the text that guarantees the reader's ethical incompleteness at the same time that the critic is inscribed as an exemplary reader (Hunter 1988a, 163). In this way, criticism, as a practice is imbedded in policies of education and paradigms of culture, is understood as a pedagogical imperative and as a system of subjective formation.

However, this triumvirate of Foucault, Bourdieu, and Hunter and the question of ethics and criticism require some further explanation. By criticism, I refer to the analysis, evaluation, and interpretation of texts; also, I refer to a form of practical criticism: a criticism in which the text is a vehicle for ethical practice, a criticism in which criticism is a mode of focusing a relation of the self to the world and others. Practical criticism is, on the one hand, criticism in a hermeneutic tradition in which interpretation becomes a pursuit of understanding, where understanding is an epistemological and ontological phenomenon embodying a historical being in the world (I will return to the question of hermeneutics) (Palmer 1969, 10). On the other hand, practical criticism is an expansion of Romantic criticism in which criticism functions as a specific cite of ethical subjectification (Hunter 1988a, 226; and Siebers 1988).

Admittedly, Romantic criticism, and better yet Romanticism, is a complex set of discourses and practices. Romanticism as an artistic movement is often seen as a reaction to Enlightenment thinking, against a culture of rationalism, a reaction valuing change, diversity, individuality, and imagination. In addition, the word "romantic," when used in reference to texts and criticism, has indeed come to signify a derision of sorts. Furthermore, Romanticism(s) as a literary and art movement is associated with the divisions of civilized and primitive, pastorality, natural genius and artistic imagination, and Rousseauan noble savagery, to name a few. However, I note that the varying connotations, the cultural derision and ambiguity directs attention to the complexity and potential multiplicity of Romanticism as a movement and as a mode of reading. It is in the complexity of Romanticism as a reaction to Enlightenment thought, as a mode of reconciliation, and in the notions of divisions,—divisions of the self and other, primitive and civilized, and the divided and the whole—which I find appropriate for my objects of study.

As noted earlier, I expand on and operate in Mills' challenge to Kant's notion of the ideal person. Implicit in the notion of the ideal person is the division of *homo phaenomenon* and *homo noumenon;* this division is simultaneously a temporal and spatial division. Ever further, I place the question of racial sub-personhood onto the division of gender, and its multiplicities. The Romantic notion of practical criticism lends itself to these discussions of dualism and race and gender and is descriptive of dual, alienated selves. Furthermore, in reference to the "twoness" of double consciousness, the similarities are more than descriptive in that they are linked philosophically to Romanticism and American Transcendentalism.

However, there lie some differences between the Romantic notion of double consciousness (or, in general, duality, two souls, two selves, etc.)

and that of DuBois. In the Euro-American Romantic and Transcendental tradition, double consciousness and duality are seen as tensions between the individual and society; alienation of the individual from the self is codified as alienation from nature (Allen 1997, 51–54; and Campbell 1987, 172–201). Alienation and the pursuit of pleasure are given virtue and moral fortitude as renewal and reconciliation between the individual and nature (Campbell, 93).

In contrast, DuBois' notion, though emerging in the same *Zeitgeist*, constructs duality and double consciousness as a racial problem, alienation is predicated upon racial difference. The two selves of DuBois' double consciousness are "warring ideals," "unreconciled." Double consciousness provides one with a way of seeing/mode of reading, with a particular vantage point and insight into the social functions and masking of whiteness:

> Of them ["the souls of white folk"] I am singularly clairvoyant. I see in and through them. I view them from unusual points of vantage. Not as a foreigner do I come, for I am native, not foreign, bone of their thought and flesh of their language. Mine is not the knowledge of the traveler or the colonial composite of dear memories, words and wonder. Nor yet is my knowledge that which servants have of master, or mass of class, or capitalist of artisan. Rather I see these souls undressed and from the back and side. I see the working of their entrails. I know their thoughts and they know that I know. This knowledge makes them now embarrassed, now furious! They deny my right to live and be and call me misbirth! My word is to them mere bitterness and my soul, pessimism. And yet as they preach and strut and shout and threaten, crouching as they clutch at rags of facts and fancies to hide their nakedness, they go twisting, flying by my tired eyes and I see them ever stripped,—ugly, human (1920, 923).

As Cornell West (1989) notes, for DuBois double consciousness is the cause of a problem: how to be American, how to resolve the "Negro problem" (142). Double consciousness, as a problem of national and ethnic identity and a subjective problematic of existence, instantiates a critique of the practice of American and European ideals of humanity and equality as practices which service the construction of whiteness, as practices which are deployed in hegemonic racial codes. For, it is not the ideals themselves, but the realization of these ideals in social hierarchies of race that double consciousness sees critically.

Furthermore, it is the "gift" of black folk that exposes the hypocrisy of practice. Ernest Allen (1997) notes that DuBois draws on Alexander

Crummell and Johann Herder's notion of the gift and is, on the one hand, an offering to American culture, an offering which would in turn reveal valued racial characters and ideals (59). On the other hand, one may also see the gift as it is embodied in the cultural practitioners and in the cultural production and artifact (for example DuBois' discussions of the Negro Spirituals and the black artist and intellectual) (Allen 1997; and DuBois 1903a and 1897). In other words, for example, with the two DuBoisian notions of the Talented Tenth as a body of intellectuals (a select few who are given the charge of racial representation and uplift in the public sphere) and the responsibility of the black artist as cultural critic (as a "co-worker in the kingdom of culture"), criticism and critical aesthetics are implicit in cultural production.[9]

Thus, I have turned to DuBois. His configuration of the experience of race as a problem forms an ethical dilemma and an awareness of ethical incompleteness. With twoness, dual selves, and the critical vision of double consciousness, the Romantic *telos* of reconciliation and restoration of the subject continuous with nature and history is rendered discontinuous, unrestorative, more critical and more directed toward ambivalence as a state of opposition and ethical critique. Ethical incompleteness is turned toward discourses of race and humanity, inscribing the bearer of the gift to be an exemplar of ethics and racial ideals. In a discursive field of blackness, double consciousness, as a mode of reading, as a hermeneutic device, is a technology of the self in negotiation with technologies of power. The figure of blackness embodied (in a given male and female body) is in negotiation with discourses of race and gender.

I should emphasize that I make no effort to value what I have called "figures of blackness" or the various cultural productions or artifacts under discussion. Instead, my project is an elaboration and evaluation of the efficacy of modes of gender and race as they inspire and promote ethical identities and practice. In this way my project is similar to Hazel Carby's (1998) discussions of DuBois and other "Race Men":

> In *The Souls of Black Folks,* DuBois's initial premise was that black people and black cultural forms did not exist in opposition to national ideals but, on the contrary, embodied those ideals. He thus attempted to rewrite the dominant cultural and political script by transferring the symbolic power of nationalism, of Americanness, into a black cultural field and onto the black male body. Mediating his concepts of race and nation, I argued, is the concept of gender, woven into a complex philosophical discourse which sought to resolve anxieties about the formation of black intellectual manhood.

I suggest that the process of imaginatively incorporating black cultural
forms into the national cultural community through the figure of black
male produces a number of significant cultural and political contradictions (45).

Carby continues to examine "a number of significant and political contradictions" of the black male as questions in the reproduction of Race Men (25).
My project is aligned with that of Carby's. Within the framework of the
problematic of ethical masculinities, Race Men are but one type of racialized
gender formation, but one type of masculinity. I propose to expand and build
upon the concept of Race Men through explication of masculinity not only
as a gender and racial ideal but also as an ethical ideal. Indeed, part of my
argument is that in practice the sets of ideals are interconnected and interde-
pendent upon one another. I use DuBois' concepts of double consciousness
and the veil in consideration of Carby's work on the legacy of DuBois as a
Race Man and exemplary masculine figure. Carby warns:

> While double-consciousness is, indeed, a product of the articulation
> between race and nation, I would argue that we need to revise our
> understanding of how this double-consciousness works in order to
> understand how gender is an ever-present, though unacknowledged,
> factor in this theory. For DuBois, the gaining of the 'true self-conscious-
> ness' of a racialized and national subject position is dependent upon
> first gaining a gendered self-consciousness (37).

For my purpose, double consciousness as a hermeneutic of duality, an
umbrella of sorts, describes a large framework under which I examine notions
of difference, dual selves, and split subjectivities. In this manner, double consciousness is a broader category which informs the discussions of racial difference as well as gender and sexual differences. For as Henry Louis Gates
(1989) notes, with double consciousness, while seeing through the veil:

> This refracted public image is distinct from the black self-image within
> his or her own cultural sphere of existence, one that is paradoxically
> separate and distinct from yet fundamentally related to white American
> culture. Nevertheless, it demands that blacks veil or mask their cultural
> selves whenever they cross or enter into the larger public discourse,
> engaging in a shared ethnic or cultural schizophrenia (xxi).

I suggest a generalization of the veil and cultural schizophrenia on a
scale beyond race and ethnicity. I suggest that the veil of double consciousness

is a trope of a subjective formation that is in negotiation between interiority and exteriority as they inform the practice and display of public image and personae, as a strategy of reading the simultaneity and intersectionality of gender and race.[10]

## RACE AND GENDER

The concept of race has been rigorously critiqued as an essence, an ethnic or national identity and as a social construct. The concept of race which I negotiate throughout my work is one which falls into a middle ground, a ground on which race is viewed as a social construct with no essential or biological/natural value, yet, as a contemporary social construct, one which is embedded in its historical origins in 18th and 19th century natural science, anthropology and philosophy (Gossett 1963; Lott 1999; West 1982, 47–65; and Young 1995). I allow no value to biological notions of race; at the same time, due to these biological notions and their histories, I must attend to their sedimentations and their social, political, and moral valences. I assume a position similar to that of Mills (1998 and 1997), one with which the concept of race is not fully dispensed, nor is it deployed as a category of biology or nature. Mills is writing in a negotiated space of "race" debates which either affirm the need for the continued discussion of race as an essence (Outlaw 1996) or refuse the category of race as pseudo-science and social construction without acknowledging or providing ways of examining the continued social relevance of race (Appiah 1992; and Zack 2000 and 1997). From Mills' position, what may be theorized as natural or biological from an essentialist standpoint is, in fact, a process of socialization and racialization based on difference. In this way race is rendered conceptual as a phenomenal difference, which belies no essential biological or natural difference. Thus, maintaining race as conceptual difference allows for a more rigorous address of its everyday challenges and repercussions.

This is indeed a fine line. For to conceptualize race as a phenomenal difference runs the risk of further essentializing race in the body, yet it is the very body which signifies race. Therefore, in attending to the body as a body disciplined by race and in discussing race and performativity as a practice of the lived-body and "experience" of blackness, my use of the concept of race is also informed by the methodology and conceptual terminology of Lewis Gordon (2000; 1997a and b; and 1995a and b). Gordon uses existential phenomenology as a hermeneutic model in his investigations of race (1995a, 5–6). Drawing on Sartre and Fanon, Gordon explores racialism and racism as acts of bad faith. In Sartrean terms, bad faith is a lie to oneself, a flight from freedom and responsibility (Sartre 86–96); furthermore, "It [bad faith] presupposes my existence, the existence of the *Other,* my existence *for* the Other, and the existence of the other *for* the other" (88). Bad faith is situational, intersubjective and contingent.

Gordon uses the notion of bad faith as a tool to examine anti-black racism and responsibility:

> Bad faith is the effort to hide from human reality, the effort to hide from ourselves. From the standpoint of bad faith, racism is the ossifi-cation of human reality into a monadic entity identical with any one aspect of its assumed duality. The racist is a figure who hides from himself by taking false or evasive attitudes toward people of other races. The antiblack racist is a person who holds these attitudes toward black people. What is the nature of these attitudes? The answer to this question will afford us a hermeneutic of antiblack racism (1995a, 94).

Though Gordon's account of existential phenomenology draws on Sartre in efforts to attend to the experience of blackness and the responsibility and ethics of racism, I, in addition, elaborate certain phenomenological concepts in reference to Merleau-Ponty (1964). I use Merleau-Ponty and his particular engagement with phenomenology because of its attention to the body and ontology and their centrality to methodology. As Merleau-Ponty notes, "the phenomenological world is not the bringing to explicit expression of a pre-existing being, but the laying down of being" (xx). And in the "laying down of being," one finds that the body,

> . . . is the vehicle of being in the world, and having a body is, for a living creature, to be intervolved in a definite environment, to identify oneself with certain projects and be continually committed to them (Merleau-Ponty, 82).

The advantage of phenomenology is in the attention to the body and embodiment; "bodily schema;" the lived-body; and the body seeing, the body seen and the body being seen.[11] These concepts engage the visibility of the body and the phenomenal differences as questions of the experience of race and as questions of critical ontology.[12] This allows me to attend to the "situatedness of human existence" as it concerns the disciplinary practices of race, the body, and the racialized body; it, furthermore, allows for questions of intentionality in racial presence and otherness to be framed as modes and meaning of being and experience.

In a fashion similar to the concept of race, gender has also been rigorously critiqued within the same debates of essentialism and social constructivism. Gender is traditionally posited as natural and biological: idealizations of masculinity and femininity are fixed in social dis-equilibrium by sex-type and (hetero)sexual function, given to the roles of men and women. However, gender—its naturalness, stability and fixity as a type and role—has been brought into question on several fronts. Social constructivism provided an early paradigm for the re-thinking of gender. Often characterized in an essentialist debate, social constructivism theorizes gender as a social construct, a construct in which "gender" is embedded in and articulated from a set of social relations, has a specific historicity, is culturally specific and is not fixed as a category.

However, these early formulations of gender sparked debates and influenced other lines of thought in cultural theory. I am speaking of feminist critiques of feminism; women of color and critical race theory's critique of feminism; and the influence of feminism on queer theory. The first two critiques of feminism, by feminists, women of color and both, raise questions of the object of feminism and feminist theory. Both critiques question the construction of woman at the expense of women. These critiques center on the divergences and discrepancies between woman as sexed and gendered and women as racial and class formations.[13] Questions of race and class broadened the social relations theorized as mediations in the social construction of gender. As racial and class formations gender can be seen in social function as hierarcharized; femininty and masculinity then become femininities and masculinities. Furthermore, as Teresa de Lauretis (1987) notes, the femininity that had been theorized earlier was, indeed, a heterosexual femininity, adding the lens of sexuality to the examination of gender and gendering.

Queer theory, as influenced by feminist theory, continues a theorization of masculinity and femininity, but broadly shifts the focus from the construction of gender and gender roles to the practice and performance of gender as it is mediated by sexual practices. Foremost among these theorists are Eve Kosofsky Sedgwick (1990 and 1985) and Judith Butler (1993 and 1990). Sedgwick's work, through reading homosocial desire and the regulatory practices within the social functioning and formation of masculinity, suggests that feminism should include a re-thinking of masculinity. Butler's work moves beyond the construction of gender to the discursive performativity of gender and gender as a citational and re-significatory

practice. Emphasizing linguistic and psychoanalytic models of subject formations, Butler raises challenging questions of subjective agency and coalition formation in the understanding of gender performativity and the
divestiture of the fixity of gender.

In exploration and elaboration of feminist thinking, recent work, primarily by men, has taken the theoretical and critical tools of feminist theory to
deconstruct and examine masculinity.[14] The body of work to which I refer
here theorizes masculinity within the concept of hegemonic masculinity. As
the guiding concept hegemonic theory is variously defined as follows:

> Hegemonic masculinity can be defined as the configuration of gender
> practice which embodies the currently accepted answer to the problem
> of the legitimacy patriarchy (Connell 77).

or,

> Hegemonic masculinity thus refers to the social ascendancy of a partic-
> ular version or model of masculinity that, operating on the terrain of
> 'common sense' and conventional morality, defines 'what it means to
> be a man' (Hanke 1990, 233)

or,

> Hegemonic masculinity, the form of masculinity that is dominant,
> expresses (for the moment) a successful strategy for the domination of
> women, and it is also constructed in relation to various marginalized
> and subordinated masculinities (e.g. gay, black, and working-class mas-
> culinities) (Messner, 7–8).

As conceptualized hegemonic masculinity provides a model of ideal masculinity which opens, or allows for the opening of, plurality, a shift from
masculinity to masculinities.

There is, though, redundancy in the model that leaves a desire for
more complexity in the understanding of masculinity. As Robert Connell
notes, "The number of men rigorously practicing the hegemonic pattern in
its entirety may be quite small. Yet the majority of men gain from its hegemony, since they benefit from the patriarchal dividend, the advantage men
in general gain from the overall subordination of women" (79). The "quite
small" number of practicing men and the subordination of women suggest
that masculinity is hegemonic as a gender construct, further suggesting that
the site of conflict is not in hegemonic masculinity as a form, albeit the

most ideal form, of masculinity, but instead, the site of inquiry should perhaps be the hegemony of masculinity, how the hegemony of masculinity in all its forms is defined, re-defined and maintained.

Furthermore, hegemonic masculinity, at the same time it proposes to be descriptive of a type of masculinity, imposes a hegemonic construct in itself. In other words, what is simultaneous with the construction and use of the term is the creation of a hegemonic masculine ideal through the hierarchy of marginalized and subordinated. The problem, then, becomes one of theorizing without the absorption and re-formation of the same categories of gender. The model offers no new insight into the intricacies of gender production and performance. The post-structural influence on the model provides the ostensible complexity of it in the gesture towards race and class, but this model only seems to simplify the discursivity of the race and class and gender into the *telos* of the hegemonic masculine. My intention here is not to dispense fully with this model; it does provide a starting point. Additionally, a critique of this model can provide critical insight into theorizing masculinity, femininity and gender, can further aid in revealing blind spots and absences in theory and practice.

Gender debates have extended beyond feminist theory and queer theory. As the recent theories of masculinity demonstrate, these debates have permeated through the disciplines of cinema studies, media studies and literary theory. The representation of gender in the media and film, especially, has undergone some dramatic shifts. The constructedness of gender is readily acknowledged in popular media through the use of male pin-up models, drag queens as runway models and in fashion photography, and androgyny in music video and performance. In film there has been an increased reframing of the representation of the male body, from increased frontal nudity to the feminization of the male body as the object of the camera's gaze.[15] Kaja Silverman (1995) has noted of film and literature that these representation of non-phallic masculinity are indicative of a historical rupture (for Silverman, the trauma and atrocities of World War II) in the subject formation of masculinity in which there is a separation of the phallus from the penis as the naturalized bodily marker of masculinity. The dissolution of the penis as the signifier of the phallus, according to Silverman, is the ruination of masculinity, allowing for the formation and representation of alternative, less oppressive masculinities.

Yet the principal debates of masculinity remain those of issues of race, class and sexuality in the formations of masculinities. Overwhelmingly, these images of newly transformed masculinities are white: the responsible father of *Kramer vs Kramer;* the angry man of *Falling Down;* the redeemed vindicators/partners in films like *Unforgiven* or the *Lethal Weapon* series;

the neo-primitive, mythical masculinity of Robert Bly's *Iron John;* or the "beautiful boys," in their non-threatening vulnerability of *haute couture* and fashion advertisements. On the one hand, one can argue that these masculinities are not transformative, alternative or any less oppressive, that they are, in fact, part of a "backlash" of sorts. Abigail Solomon-Godeau (1995), indeed, notes in response to Silverman, that these masculinities—in their reclamation, in their redemption of masculine ideals, and in the varying feminine masculinities—are colonizations of femininity in the expansion and elasticity of masculinity, that "what has been rendered peripheral and marginal in the social and cultural realm, or actively devalued, is effectively incorporated within the compass of masculinity" (73). On the other hand—or in addition to—, in the relative absence of ethnic minority masculinities and over-representation of black masculinity as controversy and celebrity, the transformations and reclamations of masculinity, in all their avowed, knowing constructedness, are coterminous with the discourse and representation of whiteness.

Richard Dyer (1997) notes the neutrality of whiteness, as a representation, is one of the more salient features of its construction (47). That the aforementioned images of ideal masculinity render the discourse of whiteness invisible, *viz.* "neutrality," is apparent in that these images are presented as universals, as the norm within the current debates and normalizing discourses of responsibility, vulnerability, and redemption.[16] In opposition, black masculinity, in the public sphere and mass media, is wholly informed and structured in discourses of exceptionalism (athletes and black entertainers) and criminality (urban youth and crime, the endangered black man, in the debates around censorship and rap). Furthermore, these black masculinities are fully contained and disciplined in the discourse of role modeling which uncritically locates transformation, expansion, and the horizon of masculinity in debates of community responsibility (when that community is one of idealized blackness preserved in the monolith of the "black man"), containing masculinity in a public personae of manhood which is limited, and limiting, in the interrogation and expression of that manhood. Seemingly identical tropes of masculine responsibility, vulnerability and redemption are deployed and mediated by competing and conflicting discourses of race, manhood, nation, heterosexuality and morality, and it is in this web of discourse exchange, formation and dissemination that masculinities are coercively hierarchized and racialized.[17]

The popular media to which I refer are specifically film, television and music. Current debates about black masculinity, and the constructions of masculinity which they engender, mediate critical and cultural production most prominently in these popular media. Part of the argument, then, is that popular media images of black masculinity necessarily contend with public discourses of the nuclear family, morality, cultural nationalism, authenticity and criminality, that these debates about black men inform the form and content of popular images of black men and of celebrity. Furthermore, the cultural production, the forms of celebrity, and the choices of media provide sites of critical intervention from which political and ethical stances are formed and circulate.

By emphasizing public personae as they circulate in and through popular media, certain performative modes of gender and race can be posited in cultural production as cultural critique and criticism, which further allows for the formulation and construction of these public personae within a discourse of criticism and ethical subject formation. In doing this, there is some engagement with stereotyping and stereotypes, and engagement which runs throughout the project. Much of this discussion of stereotypes is in direct conversation with Donald Bogle's (1988; 1980; and 1973) work on African Americans in film, but this is also informed by Ella Shohat and Robert Stam's (1994) discussions of the limits of stereotypes and positive imagery debates. Therefore, on the one hand, there is a shift from a focus on positive and negative image debates, and on the other hand, there is a widening of the critical lens under which the construction of gender, and the learning of gender roles and types, can be examined as they are mediated by constructs and notions of race and as they engage in forming and displaying ethical categories of gendered subjectivities.

Though I do emphasize the historical contexts of the emergence of particular cultural practices and the historical specificity of the objects of gender and race, I do not attempt to construct a history of race and gender in popular media. Therefore, rather than a linear and continuous argument, the various methodologies are deployed in a manner which is intertextual and conflictual, with the hope that one method informs and critiques the other in analysis of the objects under consideration. Guiding and uniting the use of these various methodologies is the discursive continuum of questions of difference and subjective formations. It is not just a question of duality, dyads, and dualisms, but—as I have tried to address through the use of concepts like "simultaneity" and "intersectionality"—one of multiplicity, perspectives and contingencies.

The arrangement is topically organized in a manner in which the different methods of analysis are used to approach the topic across the different media of film, television, and music. The discontinuity of method and argument is desired in the examination of the different texts. Different orders of discourse are necessary in the elaboration of the internal logic and self-understanding of these texts, as well as in the external interrogation, interpretation, and understanding of them. In other words, the cultural phenomena outlined require that one manipulate continuity and discontinuity in the frameworks of gender, race, and ethics in contemporary American culture.

Chapter One

# Spooks in the Mirror: Racial Performativity and Black Cinema

[T]he Negro community has been forced into a matriarchal structure which, because it is so out of line with the rest of the American society, seriously retards the progress of the group as a whole, and imposes a crushing burden on the Negro male and, in consequence, on a great many Negro women as well.

—Daniel Patrick Moynihan

By cool pose we mean the presentation of self many black males use to establish their male identity. Cool pose is a ritualized form of masculinity that entails behaviors, scripts, physical posturing, impression management, and carefully crafted performances that deliver a single, critical message: pride, strength, and control. Black males who use cool pose are often chameleon-like in their uncanny ability to change their performance to meet the expectations of a particular situation or audience. They manage the impression they communicate to others through the use of an imposing array of masks, acts, and facades.

—Richard Majors and Janet Mancini Billson

The two opening quotes are indicative of two overlapping discourses of black men. The first, from the "Moynihan Report" (1965), established the latter part of the twentieth century's discussions of black families as sites of "dysfunction"; pre-figured the governmental and media language collapse of the un-wed mother and single female-headed households onto the black family as the black un-wed mother and black single female-headed households; initiated public discussion, debates and policy geared toward the recuperation and assimilation of the black family; and pathologized blackness, laying the discursive foundations for the social categories of the inner city and underclass. "The Moynihan Report" is a re-iteration of discursive black masculinity as part of governmental policy, imposing a split image of a historical burden to the family, the economy and the nation *and* victim of institutionalized and *de facto* racism:

> When Jim Crow made its appearance toward the end of the 19th century, it may be speculated that it was the Negro male that was the most humiliated thereby; . . . and just as important, segregation, and the submissiveness it exacts, is surely more destructive to the male than to the female personality . . . Keeping the Negro 'in his place' can be translated as keeping the Negro male in his place (Moynihan, 16).[1]

Black men are *ultra*-victims, of sorts. The survival of the black man is pitted against that of the matriarchal black family that is complicit in his emasculation. The report sets the primacy of the image of the black man as the focal point of the rhetoric of race, the black family, and black women. Indeed, the black man is synecdochal in that the black man and discussion of the black man form the whole discussion of "the race" (Beavers 1997, 257). Furthermore, through the language of racial liberalism this black man is historically damaged, appealing to an American ethos of democracy and self-help that engenders a discourse of endangerment and loss.

The second quotation above is taken from *Cool Pose,* the influential study of black men. In *Cool Pose,* Majors and Billison (1992) examine the response of black men to the report's governmental discourse of family, race and gender responsibility and to popular discourses of black masculinity.[2] For Majors and Billson, cool pose is a performative response to the rhetorical and discursive absence/presence of black men, a shifting posture of masculine performances that is crafted by race, gender, and class. It also, according to Majors and Billison, deeply embedded psychically:

> Cool pose is a distinctive coping mechanism that serves to counter, at least in part, the dangers that black males encounter on a daily basis. As a performance, cool pose is designed to render the black male visible and to empower him; it eases the worry and pain of blocked opportunities. Being cool is an ego booster for black males comparable to the kind white males more easily find through attending good schools, landing prestigious jobs, and bringing home decent wages. Cool pose is constructed from attitudes and actions that become firmly entrenched in the black male's psyche as he adopts a façade to ward off the anxiety of second class status. It provides a mask that suggests competence, high self-esteem, control, and inner strength. It also hides self-doubt, insecurity, and inner turmoil (5).

Cool pose, as posited, suggests that masculinity is performance. The hyper-masculinity of the cool pose further asserts a violence and class specificity to a particular black man and practice of masculinity. The cool pose and Moynihan's "Report" are linked by their mutual engagement with the discourses of masculinity, black masculinity, and family. On the one hand, "The Moynihan Report" figures masculinity as an American ideal that black men fail to achieve, because of matriarchal family structures, crime, unemployment and the history of racism. On the other hand, *Cool Pose* figures a "pose," a performance of masculinity, inspired by the failure of and loss of an idealized masculinity which cannot be achieved because of the second class status of black men.[3]

Both the criminal and victimized black man and the cool posed black man are each others' shadow figures, reflecting a layered and embedded gendered racial performance, a masculine performance which emerges from a public self that confronts race at the same time that it maintains masculinity as a force of identity and control. Granted, cool pose is but one figure of black masculinity; nevertheless, as a problematic of identity, it is paradigmatic of an intersection between race and gender and performance (Beavers 1997).

## RACIAL PERFORMATIVITY

I use two notions of performance. The first refers to sets of actions which one is assigned to play (in theatre, film, music, etc.); this performance is an artist's performance (Sayre 1990). I will elaborate this more with Sidney Poitier and Blaxploitation. The second performance refers to performance as an aspect of performativity and self-presentation. For this idea of performance I draw on Judith Butler's (1993a and b; and 1990) elaboration of performativity. Butler's use of performativity describes a mode of discursivity in the production of gender. Indeed, Butler makes a distinction between performance (as theatrical performance and acting) and performativity (as a mode of discursive production).

Butler's performativity is derived from several theorists: First, the notion of the performative can be traced to linguistics and philosophy through J.L. Austin (1962) and his use of the performative as an utterance, as a speech act, as a form of authoritative speech, which in its uttering also performs an action (*e.g.,* "I promise," "I apologize," or in Austin's example of *I do,* in a wedding ceremony; utterances, which in their utterance, construct an object, the promise or apology).[4] Butler then argues that, even though there is the first person singular, "I," the performative does not presuppose or come from a subject, as much as it is a citation in a chain of citational power. In other words, for example, in the performative, "I sentence you . . . ," the "I" receives its binding power and authority, not from it subjectivity or subjective intention, but from its citation of the law which is applied from a prior authority which authorizes the "I." Or as Butler elaborates:

> If a performative provisionally succeeds . . . , then it is not because an intention successfully governs the action of speech, but only because that action echoes a prior action, and *accumulates the force of authority through the repetition or citation of a prior, authoritative set of practices* . . . [A] performative 'works' to the extent that *it draws on and covers over* the constitutive conventions by which it is mobilized. In this sense, no term or statement can function performatively without the accumulating and dissimulating historicity of force [original italics] (1993b, 18).

In other words, the performative is always a ruse of naturalness. Discursive performativity problematizes notions of agency and subjective agency because in this moment of performativity the "I" emerges as a nexus, a point in a chain of signifiers. The subject is then part of a re-signification practice, which in its very signification constitutes the subject at the same time that it conceals its constitution:

> [P]erformativity . . . consists in a reiteration of norms which precede, constrain, and exceed the performer and in that sense cannot be taken as the fabrication of the performer's 'will' or 'choice'; further what is 'performed' works to conceal, if not disavow, what remains opaque, unconscious, un-performable (1993b, 24).

Butler earlier uses this idea of discursive performativity to look at gender, arguing that gender is not constituted through an essence or self but through performativity, and specifically through gesture. Drawing on Esther Newton's (1972) work on female impersonation and Ervin Goffman's (1959) work on the presentation of the self, Butler suggests that gender's gestural enterprise creates an illusion of naturalness, interiority and gender subjectivity. Furthermore, as Harper (1994b) notes of Butler's notion of gender, as a performative, gender is disciplinary and regulatory in that the illusion of gender as an internal, natural core or self functions within the regulations of reproductive heterosexuality.

The elaboration of performativity is also, methodologically, an exploration of the Foucaultian concept of the statement and discursive formations:

This repeatable materiality that characterizes the enunciative function reveals the statement as a specific and paradoxical object, but also as one of those objects that men produce, manipulate, use, transform, exchange, combine, decompose and recompose, and possibly destroy. Instead of being something said once and for all—and lost in the past like the result of a battle, a geological catastrophe, or the death of a king—the statement, as it emerges in its materiality, appears with a status, enters various networks and various fields of use, is subjected to transferences or modifications, is integrated into operations and strategies in which its identity is maintained or effaced. Thus the statement circulates, is used, disappears, allows or prevents the realization of a desire, serves or resists various interests, participates in challenge and struggle, and becomes a theme of appropriation or rivalry" (Foucault 1972, 105).

As discursive formations, and as in performativity, statements are contingent and re-iterable within difference.[5] Foucaultian "statements," their discursivity, cultural and historical contingencies, and differential truth statements are implicit in Butler's notion of gender and performance:

*In imitating gender, drag implicitly reveals the imitative structure of gender itself—as well as its contingency.* Indeed, part of the pleasure, the giddiness of the performance is in the recognition of a radical contingency in the relation between sex and gender in the face of cultural configurations of causal unities that are regularly assumed to be natural and necessary [original italics] (Butler 1990, 137–138).

However, Butler's severe bracketing of gender away from other interconnected discourses that empower it leaves it as a concept and discursive practice that is overdetermined by and discursively bounded by sexual difference. Conceptions of race and gender meet in numerous scientific discourses, colonial discourse, and psychological discourse; in genetics and eugenics; in ideas of intelligence; and in theories of criminology, social degeneracy and pathology.[6] One of the recurring points of my discussion is that gender and race are inextricable in discussion and explanation of each other.[7]

In drawing on Butler's work on gender and performance it, therefore, becomes necessary to augment the theory of gender performativity.[8] In order to do so, I expand on performativity as racial performativity. Racial performativity is distinguished as a performance of the self and presentation of the self, as a process of socialization in which the performance of the self negotiates societal expectations and standards, as they are derived from racial and gender sedimentations. This is a slightly different idea of performativity, more akin to Goffman's notion of idealization, more a routine or ceremony (Goffman, 34–51). Racial performativity is a more subjective practice than Butler's gender performativity in that it is often more consciously deployed, more a question of intentionality and subjective agency.[9]

To clarify the distinction and overlap between gender performativity and racial performativity, it is important to note racial performativity as a critical performance of the self. Here again I draw on Goffman's "presentation of the self" in two aspects: First is his distinction in performance, especially as this performance is informed and performed in relation to external stimuli and subjective engagement of these stimuli.[10] For Goffman performance is a form of accentuation and concealment (67). As such performance is a mediated expression of standards and limitations, regulatory and restrictive. Furthermore, performance is situational involving "settings" and "fronts":

> 'Performance' [refers] to all the activity of an individual which occurs during a period marked by his continuous presence before a particular set of observers and which has some influence on the observers. It will be convenient to label as 'front' that part of the individual's performance which regularly functions in a general and fixed fashion to define the situation for those who observe the performance. Front, then, is the expressive equipment of a standard kind intentionally or unwittingly employed by the individual during his performance (22).

Goffman further constructs performance as "impression management," a dynamic, controlled mediation of the expressions individuals *give* and the expressions individuals *give off* (impressions) (2; and 238–239). In more ocular terms of race, there is the dynamic of seeing and being seen, which I insert, through the notion of the veil, into Goffman's performance. The notion of the veil as a performance mediator provides an understanding of "front" as a projection of a divided self. Indeed it is the specularity of race, the doubleness of seeing and being seen that is linked to Goffman's personal front and the ideas of accentuation and concealment. As conceived, the notion of racial performativity is an exploration and elaboration of a "personal front," a "front" which is informed by and engages the phenomenal, social, and historical legacy of racial categories:

> . . . [O]ne may take the term 'personal front' to the other items of expressive equipment, the items that we most intimately identify with

> the performer himself and that we naturally expect will follow the performer wherever he goes. As part of personal front we may include: insignia of office or rank; clothing; sex, age and racial characteristics; size and looks; posture; speech patterns; facial expressions; bodily gestures and the like. Some of these vehicles for conveying signs, such as racial characteristics, are relatively fixed and over a span of time do not vary for the individual from one situation to another. On the other hand, some of these sign vehicles are relatively mobile or transitory, such as facial expression, and can vary during performance from one moment to the next (24).

The situational aspect of Goffman's performance allows for the elaboration of the notions of front region and back region within racial performativity as sites, negotiable sites which are delimited by perceptions of racial difference. Personal front generates expectation and engages these expectations from both the perspectives of the observer and observed. In other words, the specularity of "race," racial characteristics and racial difference inform racial performativity from both sides, the sides of the seer and the seen and the seeing and the being seen, initiating performative responses of self-presentation which are reflective and expressive of received and perceived notions of race.

The most prominent instance of performance and impression management as racial performativity, thus far in the discussion, is cool pose:

> Cool pose is a carefully crafted persona based on power and control over what the black male says and does—how he 'plays' his role. For the black male who has limited control or access to conventional power or resources, cool pose is empowering. He can appear on the stage of life as competent, in control, playing to a diversity of audiences with flair and uniqueness. The act is not so much form dishonest, cunning, or manipulative motives as it is essential for continued survival (Majors and Billson, 28).

Cool pose as personal front in impression management is configured within racial performativity because of the integral, formative aspect of race as part of the "expressive equipment" of the performance.

The second aspect of Goffman's performance and impression management of use is the moral valence of performance, embedded in the performance itself.

> Society is organized on the principle that any individual who possesses certain social characteristics has a moral right to expect that others will

value and treat him in an appropriate way. Connected with this principle is a second, namely that an individual who implicitly or explicitly
signifies that he has certain social characteristics ought in fact to be
what he claims he is. In consequence, when an individual projects a definition of the situation and thereby makes an implicit or explicit claim
to be a person of a particular kind, he automatically exerts a moral
demand upon the others, obliging them to value and treat him in the
manner that persons of his kind have a right to expect. He also implicitly forgoes all claims to be things he does not appear to be and hence
forgoes that treatment that would be appropriate for such individuals.
The others find, then, that the individual has informed them as to what
is and as to what they *ought* to see as the 'is' (13).

Through the exchange of the giving and the given off, the exchange of
expression and impression, there is an evaluation of the performer as one
who, in expectation of performance, demands respect through the performance itself:

> . . . [S]ince the reality that the individual is concerned with is unper-
> ceivable at the moment, appearance must be relied upon in its stead.
> And, paradoxically, the more the individual is concerned with the real-
> ity that is not available to perception, the more must he concentrate his
> attention on appearances.
>
> The individual tends to treat the others present on the basis of the
> impression they give now about the past and the future. It is here that
> communicative acts are translated into moral ones. The impression that
> the others give tend to be treated as claims and promises they have
> implicitly made, and claims and promises tend to have moral character
> (249).

Furthermore, from the perspective of the expressive individual:

> We come now to the basic dialectic. In their capacity as performers,
> individuals will be concerned with maintaining the impression that they
> are living up to the many standards by which they and their products
> are judged. Because these standards are so numerous and so pervasive,
> the individuals who are performers dwell more than we might think in
> a moral world. But, *qua* performers, individuals are concerned not with
> the moral issues of realizing these standards, but with the amoral issue
> of engineering a convincing impression that these standards are being
> realized. Our activity, then, is largely concerned with moral matters,
> but as performers we do not have a moral concern with them. As per-

formers we are merchants of morality. Our day is given over to intimate contact with the goods we display and our minds are filled with
intimate understands of them; but it may well be that the more attention we give to these goods, then the more distant we feel from them
and form those who are believing enough to buy (251).

Therefore, the maintenance of impression establishes a stage, of sorts, for
the reciprocal expectation of a moral exchange; the very moment of performance becomes the stage. The distinction in the notion of blackness and
racial performativity as it is augments Goffman's notion of performance is
that, from the expressive individual's perspective, the performance and the
stage of the performance is racialized. Since it is one of the basic con-
tentions of my project that racial discourse, racial categories, and racialist
thinking pre-figure a moral and ethical dilemma, the moment of "amoral"
engineering, contrary to Goffman, is a foregrounding moment, a moment
of estrangement in the moral machinery of performance which brings to
fore the problem of the moral constructs themselves embedded in the performative equation of expression and impression.

At this point a greater discussion of race in relation to performance is
necessary. As I noted earlier, by race I do not imply an essential or biological
fact, yet the *phenomenal* difference of race remains present. Race is deeply
embedded in everyday life, identity and self-reflection, yet does not adhere
as a natural fact (though it is, indeed, often naturalized). In an effort to
understand the subjective implications of race, I follow Craig Vasey's (1999)
analogy of static and dynamic meanings of race to that of the sex/gender
difference (or in Vasey's words, " . . . race is to color as gender is to sex").
Static meanings are those whose meanings are derived from color (which I
describe as phenomenal differences); dynamic meanings are those meanings
made out of the difference of color. Even further, in keeping with this analogy, static meanings of color (as analogous to sex) are ahistorical against
the dynamic meanings of race, which are thoroughly historical (3). In
Fanonian terms, static meanings are determined by the "fact of blackness"
and dynamic meanings emerge through attached lived and subjective meanings of racial distinction. Dynamic meanings imply a mode of intentionality
which engages the situated, historical specificity of a person (Vasey, 4).

Also, important to racial performativity is the theory of signifyin(g).
As outlined by Gates (1988 and 1987), signifyin(g) is repetition with a difference. Gates' theory of signifyin(g) emerges as an exchange between
African American vernacular tradition and African American literary tradition with signifyin(g) forming a meta-discourse about literary discourse and
signification itself. In signifyin(g), the sign, what is signified, is doubled.[11] It

must be emphasized that it is through the process of signifyin(g) that the signifier is doubled, encoding the signifier in a double meaning, or a double relationship to meaning.

In addition, there is a distinction between signification and Significa-tion ["signifyin(g)"]. [s]ignfication (with the lower case *s*) denotes, *viz.* Saussure, the meaning conveyed in a term (1988, 47). [S]ignification (*S* is capitalized), on the other hand, denotes a process that is discursive and meta-critical of signification itself. Gates argues that black folk use empties out the signifier—in signification—and " . . . substituted as its concept a signified that stands for a system of rhetorical strategies . . . Rhetoric, then, has supplanted semantics in its most literal metaconfrontation within the structure of the sign" (47). *The signification of the process of signification* in signifyin(g) is no longer a semantic process, but is now a figurative and tropological praxis:

> Where as in standard English usage signification can be represented *sig-nifier/signified* and that which is signified is a concept, or concepts, in the black homonym, this relation of semantics has been supplanted by a relation of rhetoric, wherein the signifier "Signification" is associated with a concept that stands for the rhetorical structures of the black ver-nacular, the trope of trope that is Signifyin(g) (48).

In this shift from semantic to rhetorical, the sign is demonstrated to be mutable and conceptual; denotation is disrupted, doubled; signifyin(g), then, as the process for the doubling, mediates the mutability of the sign as a method of interpretation and revision.

Gates posits black oral and literary traditions as double-voiced and sig-nifyin(g), with the trope of the "talking book" as a unifying metaphor (1988, xxv). He goes further to elaborate the four double-voiced textual relations: 1). tropological revision, the repetition of a particular trope with difference, the revision of a given trope; 2). the speakerly text, one which is exemplified by the textual play of "voices" through the use of "free indirect discourse" (dialect), a discourse which deploys the direct discourse of a speech commu-nity; 3). talking texts, which are a form of intertextuality, texts which are in dialog with each other; and 4). re-writing the speakerly texts, which is a rever-sionary textual engagement with a speakerly text (xxv-xxvii). With the textual relationship of "re-writing the speakerly text," Gates makes a distinction between parody and pastiche. Parody is a motivated signifyin(g), a significa-tion other texts, a "close reading," of sorts, emphasizing critique and differ-ence. Pastiche is an unmotivated signifyin(g), a signification of other texts with the absence of negative critique (1988, 107–111; and 1987, 235–276).

Though Gates describes signifyin(g) as a concept of language and literature, signifyin(g) as a practice of difference and repetition extends beyond literature.[12] It is with these last notions of motivated parody and unmotivated parody, or pastiche, that I would like to link to racial performativity. Indeed, one may argue that signifyin(g) is racial performativity. My argument is that it is a form of racial performativity, albeit a pervasive and intertextual one. The shift from written words to the performativity of race as an embodied aesthetic practice adds a valence of corporeality, which can expand signifyin(g) as a hermeneutic device, as a mode of intentionality, which can convey a more holistic approach to understanding blackness as a symbolic and cultural signifier.[13]

Furthermore, signifyin(g) offers a master rhetorical trope within racial performativity (similar to the manner in which Butler uses drag and cross dressing), guiding the network of tropes under it (especially the figurations of metaphor, metonymy, metalepsis, and synecdoche), connecting questions of race and performativity to each other. The emphasis on rhetoric is important here because as a rhetorical strategy signifyin(g) is distinguished as persuasion and performance, has an implicit audience, and is determined in expressive style. As such signifyin(g) contains intentionality in utterance which can be addressed as style, theatricality, and fidelity to text or convention. Performance, in a traditional and rhetorical sense, is given as public address. At the same time, the performance of signifyin(g) lends itself to the discursivity of performativity in that the signifyin(g) performance is also a critical *re-presentation* and *redress* in parody of "statements," a critical appropriation of discourse.

To return to the example of cool pose, as racial performativity and an instance of signifyin(g), cool pose is often configured as style and stylized behavior:

> The expressive life-style transforms the mundane to the sublime and makes the routine spectacular. It is a dynamic rather than a static art form characterized by such new aesthetics as rap music, 'the cabbage patch dance,' and breakdancing (Majors and Billson, 70).[14]

With closer examination, the stylization of black masculinity in cool pose, the strategic use of style as a coping device, raises the practice as a question of signifyin(g). Cool pose provides a troping, a performative appropriation of masculine ideals, which in the double speak of signifyin(g), presents and re-presents masculinity, through the presentation of gender as something attained and maintained, and through the re-presentation of gender as racial authority, control and strength. The slippage in the signifyin(g) re-articulation of masculinity foregrounds masculinity as a construct and process which is determined not only by sex-type, but also by racial valuations of gender itself, by the discourse of race. Cool pose, as a re-articulation of masculinity, is signi-fyin(g), is a mechanism for coping:

> The purpose of posing and posturing—being cool—is to enhance social competence, pride, dignity, self-esteem, and respect. Cool enhances mas-culinity. Being cool also expresses bitterness, anger, and distrust to ward the dominant society for many years of hostile mistreatment and discrim-ination. Cool pose helps keep the dominant society off balance and puz-zled and accentuates the expressive self (Majors and Billson, 105).

Racial performativity describes a racial parody in which the differ-ence of race, the static meaning of color, is given privileged, critical agency.[15] It is an imitation with a critical difference in its repetition. If, for example, I state that black masculinity is a racial performance, I suggest that this discursive figure engages in a repetition and revision of the social constructs of race and gender. Black masculinity as a repetition is a replica-tion of idealized norms (whiteness and masculinity) in the non-ideal field of blackness. Unlike gender parody, which Butler (1990) discusses in the con-text of compulsory heterosexuality, racial performativity is a more fluid, intentional performance. However, continuing with the example of black masculinity, that racial performance is always a simultaneous gender per-formance imposes interdictions that render the racial performance polemi-cal, or at least ambivalent, in relation to racial ideals.[16] In other words, race and gender as discursive formations in the context of a gendered and racial-ized social structure support each other in discourse and citational perform-ances, at the same time that they contradict each other (as in the constructions and social functions of ideal types in the forms of the non-ideal types of black men).[17] Racial performativity in the disjuncture of par-ody serves to reveal inconsistencies, cracks and fissures, and ruptures in the fixity of the constructs of race and gender.

Admittedly, the notion of racial performativity is an instance of "strategic essentialism," a reification of sorts of the discursive functions of race and gender, in an effort to produce a critique of race and its discursive functions.[18] It becomes necessary simultaneously to posit race within its history of static meanings in order to critique it as process, as performance with dynamic, multiple (and multiplying) meanings. Once one moves beyond the moment of essentialism, one is able to mobilize racial con-structs as racial performativity, in that blackness is able to be conceived as a tool, as a device of interpretation, albeit one with a historical origin. With this understanding performativity not only provides a framework for corporeal, ceremonial, and linguistic acts, but also for more dynamic signifying practices such as cinema and film viewing.

## RACIAL PERFORMATIVITY AND BLACK CINEMA

> Usually, *The Birth of a Nation* is discussed in terms of its contributions to cinemas technique, but as with every other technical advance since the oceanic sailing ship, it became a further instrument in the dehumanization of the Negro. And while few films have gone so far in projecting Negroes in a malignant light, few before the 1940's showed any concern with depicting their humanity. Just the opposite. In the struggle against Negro freedom, motion pictures have been one of the strongest instruments for justifying some white Americans' anti-Negro attitudes and practices. Thus the South, through D.W. Griffith's genius, captured the enormous myth-making potential of film form almost from the beginning. While the Negro stereotypes by no means made all white men Klansmen the cinema did to the extent that audiences accepted its image of Negroes, make them participants in the South's racial ritual of keeping the Negro 'in his place'
>
> —Ralph Ellison, "The Shadow and the Act"

To discuss images of African Americans in Hollywood film, one site with which to begin is D.W. Griffith's *The Birth of a Nation* (1914). Indeed, there are other historical sites with which to begin[19]; however, *Birth of a Nation* inspires such importance in that it serves not only as the introduction of a form and style of narrative film, but also as the successful adaptation and introduction of an economy of images and cultural archetypes of blackness to the then new film form, the feature film. Furthermore, the production and longevity of the images and feature form are indicative of the function and cultural instrumentality of popular film itself, or as Ellison continues further to note:

> To direct an attack upon Hollywood would indeed be to confuse portrayal with action, image with reality. In the beginning was not the shadow, but the act, and the province of Hollywood is not action, but illusion. Actually, the anti-Negro images of the films were (and are) acceptable because of the existence throughout the United States of an audience obsessed with an inner psychological need to view Negroes as less than men. Thus, psychologically and ethically, these negative images constitute justifications for all those acts, legal, emotional, economic and political, . . . The anti-Negro image is thus a ritual object of

which Hollywood is not the creator, but the manipulator. Its role has been that of justifying the widely held myth of Negro unhumanness and inferiority by offering entertaining rituals through which that myth could be reaffirmed (Ellison 1953, 276–277).

Ellison's comments may be dated to a critique of the Jim Crow South and post-World War II images of African Americans, but still his comments register the manner in which film as a popular medium engages national discourse and mythmaking for the discursive transcoding of other culturally coded images, narratives and histories. Griffith's mastery of the technology and apparatus of cinematic form (continuity editing, close-up, parallel action shots, pans, tracking shots) produces a narrative form unique to cinema, at the same time that it is the instantiation of an epic re-presentation of a national narrative. The visual codes of blackness in early Hollywood are given to the service of narrative convention, relying not only on the tradition of blackface and minstrelsy, but also on literary figuration of blackness. In other words, *Birth* receives the attention as a classic text because of its then unique manipulation of film's formal and technological properties, while building on existing narratives of race and nation. Furthermore, in this nexus of innovation and instantiation, *Birth* initiated and aggravated a long standing debate about the representations of Africa-Americans in film and control and production of these representations, providing a seminal, foundational film text to which these images can be mapped and traced.[20]

The repercussions of *The Birth of a Nation* are, therefore, both political and aesthetic. When considering the cultural instrumentality of film as a cinema of illusion—as well as a standardized entertainment commodity of mass consumption—, one concurs with Diawara as he notes that *Birth* provides a "master text," a "grammar book for Hollywood's representation of Black manhood and womanhood," instituting "a ban on African Americans' participation in the bourgeois humanism on Hollywood screens" (1993, 3–4). Metaphors of blackness, literary and visual, are metonymically linked to the body of actors, altered in blackface, linking "race" and blackness to costume, pose, gesture, and cinematic technique of lighting and editing in the conventional form of the narrative feature film. In the cinematic reproduction of reality, the national narratives of the Reconstruction, slavery, and race engender a discursive denial of humanity in technology and narration, a denial in the apparatus and story.[21]

Thomas Cripps (1977) notes that in response to the outcry against *Birth* early twentieth century black public figures and civic groups urged for the production of black films, films written and directed by and about

African Americans. Speaking here of one such group, Lincoln Motion Picture Company, Cripps writes:

> They shared the common goals of producing movies with black investments in the plot-lines, black characterizations with humane dimensions, dramatic conflict based upon the facts of American racial arrangements, and a conscious effort to make the tools of the filmmaker speak to black needs. Together they represented the first measurable black efforts to challenge the white monopoly over the art of cinema (70).

What emerges, motivated by the success of and protest to *Birth,* are the political and aesthetic foundations of Black Cinema. In this instance, Black Cinema relies on a long, documented history of black cultural and economic nationalism present from the Abolitionist Movement, through the Harlem Renaissance and Black Arts Movement, to contemporary New Black Cinema. In these early visions of Black Cinema, there is an investment in cultural production of the prospect of racial uplift and the ascent to public humanity and cultural and popular citizenship through further investing art with powers of social change and autonomy (the DuBosian "gift").[22]

However, the more contemporary notion of Black Cinema, and furthermore New Black Cinema, needs further elaboration and clarification. When I speak of Black cinema and New Black cinema, I refer to "black cinema" as an aesthetic expression and perform a periodization of production and expressive development. As an aesthetic expression black cinema is configured as a black aesthetic expression, which is informed by the materiality of struggle, is necessarily oppositional, political and historical in its construction (hooks 1990, 103–113). Or as Gladstone Yearwood (2000) notes,

> ..., a black cinema aesthetic refers to a set of values one finds in black film. These values provide a conceptual foundation for understanding art, and they establish paradigms for the making of narratives and the forms used for storytelling. They also outline the terms of engagement the artwork seeks with its primary audiences and helps establish a critical framework for evaluating art (79).

With this understanding of black aesthetics, Yearwood continues further to describe black cinema in relation to "traditional cinema,":

> Because traditional cinema functions to reproduce the acceptable legitimate positions prevalent in society, black cinema is conceived in necessary

opposition to these dominant sociopolitical structures. There is an emphasis on forms of production and influence over the productive processes of
cinema. If the practice of black cinema is derived from that of Hollywood,
then it will serve to reproduce the unequal relations characteristic of
blacks in society. Hence, the most appropriate strategy is to conceive of
black film as a specific signifying practice that proposes a different set of
historical relations of productions (84).

This explanation of black cinema is in position to be both praised and
problamatized, for the emphasis on black cinema as a signifying practice[23]
shifts the emphasis from the essentialized, Afro-centric definitions of black
films as those necessarily made by a black person, onto the historical contingencies of blackness. In this way "black" refers not only to the phenomenal difference of blackness, but also to blackness as an aesthetic and
political practice and strategy. As such black film does not refer to a category of film or kind of film (so not only "those by black people"), but to an
aesthetic sensibility, indeed a signifying practice which functions as a
hermeneutic device.

At the same time Yearwood is constantly undermining the signifying
practice by further constructing black film as a genre, as a kind of film.[24]
Black film as genre, as we have seen historically in the marketing and production strategies of Hollywood studio films, limits a given film as a film
for a "black" audience, with "black" themed content and formal conventions, and is often viewed as a social problem film or more contemporarily
as a "hood" film. The category of "black film" then leads to a de-valuation
of the film itself or, as Yearwood notes, renders a film that is considered
generically black to that of the Hollywood "B" movie.

For my purpose, the importance of black film as a signifying practice
(as opposed to a textual category or a group of films), its significance in
defining black film—and divesting of the phenomenal criteria of race—is
that it renders the question of the "race" of the producer of the cultural
artifact (*i.e.*, a film) secondary if the artifact is within an aesthetic and cultural tradition of African Americana. Furthermore, the emphasis on black
film as a signifying practice allows for the emphasis of genricity[25] and the
performative interplay between the cinematic apparatus and narrative
structures and the historical and discursive constructions of race embedded
in the use of the apparatus of cinema. Indeed, this notion of black film
refers to a transgeneric expressivity which operates across genres and types
of films: black film performatively engages a singular syntactic system (that
of genre, though informed by the social history and practices of blackness
as an aesthetic expression) transforming the semantic units of a given

genre, allowing the genre itself to address the specificity of blackness. If taken to its limit, this notion of aesthetics and signifying practice can be extracted from "race" (in its socialized bodily forms, and the necessity of the person being black) and abstracted into the historical struggle of racial and social domination and opposition as an aesthetic, ethical and critical practice of cultural production.

This idea of black film is informed by Yearwood's notions of black aesthetics and conceptually and theoretically re-configures black film as an aesthetic, as an oppositional aesthetic, as a hermeneutic device for the interpretation of culture and history. The efforts to detach the definition from the body of race are efforts of inclusion, which to some extent require racial qualifications, at the same time that they—through these qualifications—move beyond categories to various histories and their interconnectedness, exchange and sedimentations. In other words, there is a *telos,* one which follows a trajectory of particular to cosmopolitan, one which necessarily starts with tradition through to the uptake and dispersal of that tradition to transgenricity.

Let me clarify: the notion of black cinema that I configure here is again another instance and deployment of "strategic essentialism" in two respects: first, I posit that as a signifying practice, black cinema emerges as a political and aesthetic response to racist imagery and as a pedagogical and critical tool and, therefore, engages the racial identitarian politics of being a practice "by, for, and about." Furthermore, in this respect, as a cinema of identity, it requires an understanding of its historical periods and evolution. In doing so, one runs the risk of constructing black cinema as a kind of film, a cinema of "black movies." As a consequence, that second strategic moment is the engagement with genre and formal convention. As the discussion of Sidney Poitier and Blaxploitation demonstrates, there is a need to engage black film as a genre, as a kind of film; at the same time, the notion of genre and black film as genre are not the limit. Through an examination of Sidney Poitier and Blaxploitation, black film is seen as a signifying practice of blackness, as aesthetic expression and opposition through racial performativity; and of the apparatus of cinema, as a tool for the expression of blackness.

Chapter Two

# "Stand up, boy!": Sidney Poitier, "boy" and Filmic Black Masculinity

Again I reference *boys*. The boy in the title of this chapter refers to the gender and racial ideal of the *boy* in the introduction. However, this is a grammatically and metaphorically contained boy, for the quotation marks ("boy") indicate certain dubiousness in the signifier, *boy*. I say dubious because "boy" also references, in this instance, the star persona of Sidney Poitier. The quotation marks are not intended to raise the doubt of Poitier as a male or black man, but, instead, the question lies in Poitier as a figure of masculinity, of the attainment of an idealized masculinity, of the status of *boy*, and of the limits of that status and its attainment.

The main title of this chapter, "Stand up, boy," is taken from *In the Heat of the Night* (Norman Jewison 1967), and it serves as the introduction to the star in a star vehicle.[1] *In the Heat of the Night* is a pivotal film in Poitier's career since it is one of the three top grossing films for 1967, one of the three top grossing films, of which Poitier appears in all three (*To Sir with Love* and *Guess Who's Coming to Dinner* are the other two top grossing films of 1967). The use of this clip of dialog is deliberately signifying on the irony of Poitier's career until that date: Poitier was able to command record salaries, have record grossing films, receive an Academy Award, yet in the formal tradition of star vehicles—a tradition which provides a character type and generic setting for the star persona, provides an opportunity for a star to relish in his or her performative persona—, Poitier is introduced as a "boy" in the derogatorily racist address of a deputy sheriff. It is the direct address, "Stand up, boy," that informs the audience of the narrative presence of a motivating character and of a performer who has achieved a star status. Granted that Mr. Tibbs, Poitier's Philadelphia police detective, is only a character and not an index of an actual person, the discursive textual address as "boy" and the paratextual discourse of stardom (as a function of a democratic ethos of achievement and equality), as well as the metatextual discourse of race, open an ironic space at the site of the signifier *boy*. It is from this ironic space that I wish to interrogate the image of Sidney Poitier and black masculinities in contemporary cinema.

The purpose of this chapter, therefore, is to examine what I posit as a moment of continuity in a seemingly discontinuous and heterogeneous array of representations of black masculinity in Hollywood film. In order to do this, I take the reader through a winding series of excursions. First, I briefly provide an understanding of filmic black masculinity, providing a framework for the understanding of the main topic this chapter. Second, I position the star persona of Sidney Poitier alongside, and against, the "superbad" black men of the Blaxploitation era. This is nothing new (see Bogle 1988; Boyd 1997; George 1994; and Guerrero 1993). In order to do this, I have chosen to discuss Poitier's first autobiography, *This Life*. This discussion requires that I provide some framework for the use and under- standing of autobiography, in particular African American autobiography. Furthermore, I consider the transition from Poitier to Blaxploitation as an expression of racial performativity and black cinema. By this I mean to consider Poitier as a singular figure in Hollywood, as a monolithic figure of the black masculine within the framework of racial performativity outlined in the preceding chapter, as an expression and instance of black cinema, and as an ethical construct of masculinity who, through his engagement with racial discourse of the era, configures a discursive dialog within black masculinity. This requires that I interrogate the monolith of Sidney Poitier, during his peak, social problem film phase, and the fashioning and his self- fashioning of race and cinema during this phase.

## FILMIC BLACK MASCULINITY

What do I mean by filmic masculinity? On a simplistic level, I mean the mas- culinity portrayed in film. However, this presupposes that there is difference between the social and the filmic. Indeed there is, the filmic form provides a spectacle of gender, spectacular and specular. Gender in film, as in other media, is a fully discursive form positioned for idealization, critique, and deconstruction. Filmic masculinity, then, is also determined by the use of film, the mode of production, the genre, aesthetics, aesthetic movements, and the historical moment, to name a few. My interest, in particular, is in filmic black masculinity. The category, or the categorization, of filmic masculinity is intended to imply dialog and discursivity. For if one constructs filmic mas- culinity as a product of society, as produced within the social for the purpose of entertainment, polemic, or document, one must consider social forms, hierarchies, and continuities and discontinuities in masculinity.

In *Toms, Coons, Mulattoes, Mammies, and Bucks,* Donald Bogle (1973) outlines a catalogue of stock character types of black men and women in the Hollywood tradition of "mainstream" film. For Bogle these five types provide the traditional codings of blackness as these codings are informed by race and gender. The types are elaborated as follows: 1). Toms: Uncle Tom figures, a literary trope, complacent, politically inactive, gendered masculine, but asexual; 2). Coons (also known as zip coon): Less docile figures than the Tom, ostentatious, descendent from the minstrel shows, entertaining black men, playful and silly; 3). Mulatta/oes: Another literary trope, transcoded and transferred to film, highly sexualized, most often female; 4). Mammy: Female Tom, of sorts, aggressively maternal, physically unattractive, usually asexual; and 5). Buck: Overly sexual, and therefore contained, black men.

Bogle argues that this economy of image types governs the representation of African Americans in film. I emphasize Bogle's work because it provides a point of reference for filmic black masculinity, a history informing my work here. Bogle's schema has its advantages: it is an exhaustive reference for blacks in film, names and titles. It offers a catalogue of stock figures, archetypes, and tropes of blackness. However, there are disadvantages: Bogle does not interrogate his cataloguing as part of the process of stereotyping that is presented. The list of figures has an essentializing motive, presupposing a racial authenticity in the inauthenticity of the images. *Toms, Coons, Mulattoes, Mammies, and Bucks* is the limit of expressions of blackness, and it, in turn, is limiting of expressions of blackness as *post-, neo-, remade,* or *re-interpretations* of the limit, never allowing the possibility of excess, engagement, dialog, or discontinuity: Every black character, in every film, black or not, is a variation of the same thing. It is my contention that *Toms, Coons, Mulattoes, Mammies, and Bucks* is a source book of imagery and types, but the source itself is to be brought into question. One way of doing this is through examining texts around films or film stars. I take on the object of some of Bogle's, and a number of other critics,' venom and disparagement, Sidney Poitier, and I do this through Poitier's own efforts at understanding his relationship to film and film history, through the paratext of autobiography.

## AUTOBIOGRAPHY AND THE ETHICAL CONSTRUCTION OF THE SELF

I use the autobiographical instead the filmic for several reasons: First, as Dyer (1986) notes, "The star phenomenon consists of everything that is publicly available about stars. A film star's image is not just his or her films, but the promotion of those films and of the star through pin-ups, public appearances, studio hand-outs and so on, as well as interviews, biographies and coverage in the press of the star's doings and 'private' life" (2–3). I have, therefore, chosen the paratext of the autobiography in an effort to understand not only the star phenomenon, but also the ethical construction of the self that emerges in the becoming of a star; second, in keeping with the public and ethical dimension of the first, there is the autobiography and the autobiographic function of the text as the construction of an exemplary figure, as an ethical construction of the self; and third, there are the specific cultural and textual ramifications of the African American autobiography: Let me elaborate.

By autobiography, I mean a retrospective narrative, a personal retrospective narrative of an individual's life—or a moment in that life (as in a political post, career, episode, etc.)—in which the interrelations between the self and the formative institutions and discourses (be they social, political, personal, or religious) are taken into account in the recounting of the life story. Indeed, this working definition of autobiography is a compilation of a number of readings of autobiography, as literary genre, as a mode of writing, and as a stylistic expression of authorial intent.[2] I do not raise the question of or emphasize the verity of autobiography; I am interested here in the function of autobiography, the use of the formal aspects of autobiography as a mode of address to an audience, as a means to an end in the exemplification of a critical self. This is, admittedly, a revisionist definition of autobiography. Deliberate and self-serving, this definition seemingly relies on Phillipe Lejuene's (1989) theories and criticisms of autobiography which emphasize the "autobiographical pact," an agreement between the author (the signer of the name) and the reader of the autobiography; and in turn, this definition seemingly ignores Paul de Man's (1984) deconstructive musings on autobiography as a figure of reading, as the "specular structure" in the text, as a linguistic structure of self-knowledge that is a function of both fiction and autobiography.[3] However, this reliance and ignorance is only seeming, for this intentional "undecidability"[4] in the given positioning of the definition of autobiography opens a space for the reading of African American autobiography in its totality as a problematic form in the autobiographic tradition. Where Lejuene's definition directs attention to an autonomous subject, to autobiography as an act of individuation, de Man disperses autobiography into figurality and the fluidity of unstable meaning between autobiography and fiction, leaving autobiography as an wholly linguistic, figural play of the textual self, without extratextual referentiality, without the possibility of an autobiographical self. Following Albert Stone's (1993) suggestions, it becomes necessary to consider African American autobiography as negotiating in an interstitial space between these two, between tradition and experiment, attending to and re-deploying both as a form of self-fashioning, self-criticism and self-liberation (188).

The history of the African American autobiography is complex and multifaceted. The African American autobiography is firmly set in the Western tradition of autobiography as a personal narrative of one's life, as the story of an exemplar, as a personal testimony. Yet, it is also part of a distinctly American tradition of Transcendentalism and pluralism. Lawrence Buell (1991) traces the most formative years of American autobiography to the American antebellum and its conflicted, Puritanical notion of the self (47–48). The self was seen in religious and autobiographical writings as something to be transcended, as a hindrance to perfection. In contrast to the solipsistic, private self of the European autobiography, the American autobiographical self sought universality through a kind of effacement of particularity. Indeed, the cultural tenants of Transcendentalism present the *I* of the antebellum autobiography as a conflicted one, one which asserts an *I* in order to erase it in universalism. As Sacvan Bercovitich (1982) suggests, in the American autobiography, the "Protestant-libertarian model of the self" ("self-effacing, exemplary and self-transcending" [142]) is in opposition to the "Rousseauseque self" (146).

Furthermore, there is the history of the African American slave narrative, which, though in the American transcendental, puritanical self tradition, served as a testament to not only the cruelty of slavery, but also to the humanity of the slave. Williams Andrews (1993a) notes of the slave narrative and the African American autobiographical tradition:

> It was the eighteenth-century slave narrator who first sang into print the 'long black song' of black America's quest for freedom. Since then African American autobiography has testified to the ceaseless commitment of people of color to realize the promise of their American birthright and to articulate their achievements as individuals and as persons of African descent. Perhaps more than any other literary form in black American letters, autobiography has been recognized and celebrated since its inception as a powerful means of addressing and altering sociopolitical as well as cultural realities in the United States (1).

And recently, in his autobiographical and theoretical writing on race and autobiography, Crispin Sartwell (1998) has argued that slave narratives, and African American autobiography broadly, challenge the epistemic regime of race by foregrounding race and strategies of racialization as questions of truth and knowledge:

> The slave narratives established a discourse of truth and knowledge. The
> persons who wrote the slave narratives brought their knowledge of the
> particular conditions of slavery to bear in an enunciation of the truth
> about slavery, and sought by this exercise to transform the conditions that
> had oppressed them. They attempted to shatter the lies in which slavery
> concealed itself by an assertion of knowledge: knowledge both of the con-
> ditions under which African Americans lived and the conditions by which
> they were oppressed. Most especially, they sought to shatter the lies that
> enshrouded not black degradation but white domination (55).

These descriptions (Stone and Sartwell's) of slave narratives assign a task to
the tradition of African American autobiography, one which positions
autobiography as a mode of social and cultural critique and as a mode of
engagement with questions of humanity and the category of the subperson.
The undecidability of autobiographical narrative form and history operates, in the context of African American autobiography, as a critical
endeavor positing the African American, the black experience, and African
American culture as a mode of counter-knowledge (Sartwell, 61).

However, this position of undecidability still leaves the notion of
African American autobiography and the chronicling of the black experience within a problematic, for this position confines the African American
autobiography and blackness, as the signifier of race, within the idea of
"black as a problem." Within this problematic, the African American autobiography does not escape its origins in slave narrative and the strategic use
of autobiography and the writing of one's own narrative as an effort to
overcome the category of the subperson, as an effort at establishing personhood and humanity. Lewis Gordon (2000) argues that the trajectory of personhood sought in the African American autobiography, indeed, stems
from an epistemic openness which encourages the possibility of personhood and humanity, but this epistemic openness is rendered as epistemic
closure with the reduction of blackness to a "problem," to essentialist
"experience" in which there is a loss of historicity and contingency:

> It is no wonder that the autobiographical medium has dominated
> black modes of written expression. The autobiographical moment
> afforded a contradiction in racist reason: How could the black, who
> by definition was not fully human and hence without a point of view,
> produce a portrait of his or her point of view? The black autobiogra-
> phy announced a special form of biography, a text that was read for
> insight into blackness, which meant that paradoxically some of the
> problems of epistemic closure continued through an engagement that

admitted epistemic possibility. The interest in black autobiography carried expectation and curiosity (23).

Epistemic closure forgoes further exploration confining the individual African American autobiography to the social role of blackness, to the exteriority of the hypervisibility of blackness as a known social problem, without the distinction or nuance of the individual experience of blackness:

> In the case of epistemic closure, however, the identification of the social role is all one needs for a plethora of other judgments. In effect, to know that role is to know all there is to know about the individual. In effect, there is no distinction between him and his social role, which makes the individual an essential representative of the entire group. The group, then, becomes pure exterior being. Its members are literally without insides or hidden spaces for interrogation. One thus counts for all. The guiding principle of avoiding the fallacy of hasty generalization is violated here as a matter of course. Blacks become both effect and cause, cause and effect, an identity without dynamism, without possibility (Gordon 2000, 88–89).

Indeed, epistemic closure is an end of the process of inquiry, a judgment of "say no more" from the "outside," as Gordon notes, from the side of critical reception, providing the limit of blackness and from the "inside" providing a limiting factor in the construction of blackness. It is as a limiting factor from which epistemic closure—the cessation of knowledge and knowledge claims in being black—that blackness is written into authenticity, into Afro-centricity and into the monologics of the individual as synecdoche (as in "It's a black thang: you wouldn't understand!").[5] In other words, Gordon's argument of whiteness performing an epistemic closure of blackness is also problematically produced in the imaginative and experiential constructions of African American autobiography by the autobiographers as well, resulting in what Henry Louis Gates (1988) has identified as the black experience as that of the transcendental signifier of the African American transcendent subject (128–29). It is my intention to demonstrate Sidney Poitier's manipulation of this autobiographical tradition to his own purpose in order to move beyond the limit of an imposed blackness and the limiting factors of an imposing blackness.

## SIDNEY POITIER THE RACE MAN

> [S]ince the dominant view holds prideful self-respect as the very essence of healthy African American identity, it also considers such identity to

be fundamentally weakened wherever masculinity appears to be com-
promised. While this fact is rarely articulated, its influence is nonetheless real and pervasive. Its primary effect is that all debates over and
claims to 'authentic' African American identity are largely animated by
a profound anxiety about the status specifically of African American
*masculinity* (Harper 1996, ix).

The book's [*The Films of Sidney Poitier*] introductory essay stated
that Poitier, though born in Miami, was reared in the Bahamas and
arrived in New York in 1943 with nothing but a thick accent and great
ambition. [ . . . ]But Sidney, whose career was built on masquerading as
an African American, successfully avoided our prejudices. The qualities
I admired in Sidney were the things that made me resent the West Indi-
ans that I knew. The irony is that a lot of the regal bearing he projected
could, in another context, have been seen as insufferable superiority
(George 1994, 17–18).

The two quotations above serve as guideposts for the following discussion
of Sidney Poitier. The first taken alongside the criticisms of Poitier at the
height of his career labels the criticisms as indicators of a crisis in the
African American identity and what Phillip Brian Harper identifies as the
"status of blackness." Nelson Gorge's comments mark yet another debate
about blackness that is lost in Poitier's image, in its singularity during the
period, but given presence by Poitier in both installments of his autobiography. This "presence," as I call it, is one of ethnicity, of an ethnic blackness
which in the monologic racial imagery of his career is silenced as a signifier
of difference, but in the self-restoration of himself in the autobiographical
form, his cultural difference from the overdetermined blackness of his film
characters is significant in understanding his model of gender and race.

*This Life* (1980), Poitier's first autobiographical installment, is a textual nexus. *This Life* is a simultaneity of narratives: it is an immigrant tale,
a migration tale, a testimonial, a confessional, a chronicling of the black
experience, a conservative "picked myself up by the boot straps tale," as
well as a liberal tale of cultural pluralism; but first and foremost Poitier's
autobiography is a star's tale and the story of a public life. As a star's tale,
*This Life* implies certain meanings and social functions. For Richard Dyer
(1986) stars are a particular expression of the individual in society: "Stars
articulate what it is to be a human being in contemporary society; that is,
they express the particular notion we hold of the person, of the 'individual.'
They do so complexly, variously—they are not straightforward affirma-
tions of individualism. On the contrary, they articulate both the promise
and the difficulty that the notion of individuality presents for all of us who

live by it" (8). Furthermore, as David P. Marshall (1997) elaborates, stardom and celebrity are expressions of a democratic ethos within which there is an oscillation between individual and collective expression of possibility in a "democratic age" (6), or as Marshall explains: "The celebrity is centrally involved in the social construction of division between the individual and the collective, and works discursively in this area. . . . Also, expansion of celebrity status in contemporary culture is dependent on its association with both capitalism, where the celebrity is an effective means for the commodification of the self, and democratic sentiments, where the celebrity is the embodiment of the potential of an accessible culture" (25–26). From these notions of the star and celebrity, one gathers that the star functions as a commodity to be consumed; however, the affective consumption of stars is through the discourse of individuality, as a contradictory expression of a collective identity. In addition, and of importance to Poitier's persona, the *telos* of individuality in the discourse of stardom is personhood, as an individual whole, as a unit in a democratic society in which stars signify possibility. Poitier demonstrates this discursive relation to stardom and personhood clearly in a modestly self-congratulatory moment:

> With the release of each of my fifteen films, my name had become increasingly familiar to filmgoers, and by the end of 1962 there was developing in Hollywood a historymaking new attitude countering the long-held conviction that the appearance of blacks in other than menial roles would offend the movie industry's principal constituency. The realization that year by year more and more white Americans were willing to pay their way into a theater to see entertainment about blacks or involving blacks would encourage most of the studios to make minor alterations in their rigid and generally insulting policy for dealing with America's black citizens. Though history will accurately acknowledge my presence in those proceedings, my contribution was no more important than being at the right place at the right time, one in that series of perfect accidents from which fate fashions her grand designs. History will pinpoint me as merely a minor element in an ongoing major event, a small if necessary energy. But I am nonetheless gratified at having been chosen (*TL*, 241).[6]

It is clear here that the notion of the individual person as a success has a community relation, at least for Poitier, which is tempered by the notion of race. The discursive personhood of stardom is embedded in the trajectory of personhood which mediates the function and mode of address of the self in African American autobiographic tradition. Upon closer examination the sense of communal self present in the quote above becomes integral in understanding the ethical and exemplary self put forth by the autobiography. This requires a closer look at the individual and personhood in stardom.

In the discourse of stardom, personhood is most prominently articulated through the dichotomy of public and private. It is no wonder that as the story of a public life, Poitier's *This Life* is a private story. With stars and celebrities, private *versus* public provides a framework for the negotiation of a set oppositions, among which is the individual *versus* the collective, but also the sincere *versus* insincere, country *versus* city, racial *versus* ethnic, among them (Dyer 1986, 11).[7] Drawing on the distinction between the private/public dichotomy, Marshall (1997) adds: "This disintegration [between private and public] as represented by celebrities, has taken on a particular form. The private sphere is constructed to be revelatory the ultimate site of truth and meaning for any representation in the public sphere" (247). As a consequence the star biography or autobiography becomes a revelation of a private self.[8]

The star autobiography has, like the autobiographical form in general, truth claims, in this instance, truth claims to the "realness," the somewhat combatively real story of a star's life. The star autobiography is, on the one hand, a constructed, narrative self-representation; and, on the other, it is an answering to criticism of the public image, a projection of another truth claim, a true persona, to counter the film persona, the star type. This answering is mediated across the private/public divide, as confessional of or testimony to a private self, perhaps in opposition to or celebration of the public self that is the star.

In the case of Poitier, considering that the autobiography arrives some ten to fifteen years after the height of his career (as opposed to writing his autobiography in 1967 or the early Seventies), the mediation of the private/public sets of opposition perform a self-restoration of his image in certain capacities. In the chapter entitled "Black Films," Poitier discusses the private shock of the public proclamation against him, the *New York Times Article*, "Why do white folks love Sidney Poitier so?" by Clifford Mason:

> At about that time [1969, near the time of the release of *The Lost Man* (Robert Alan Arthur, 1969)] Clifford Mason, a writer who dabbled at playwriting in community theaters, got an assignment from the *New York Times* to write an article on me. It was called 'Why Do White Folks Love Sidney Poitier So?' It was the most devastating and unfair piece of journalism I had ever seen. When I read it, I said to myself: This definitely signaled a bad period for me. On that Sunday morning I was convinced that the brick-by-brick growth of my career was complete—it had

peaked, and there was no place to go but down. In that article Clifford Mason ripped to shreds everything I had ever done. He ripped up *In the Heat of the Night,* and the character I played in particular, to show why white people thought I was so terrific, why they made me such a 'big star.' Then he went on to destroy *To Sir With Love* and *Guess Who's Coming to Dinner*—and then he went further back into my career and proceeded to skin me alive retroactively. I was an 'Uncle Tom,' 'a lackey,' 'a house Nigger'—current terms for a lot of people, including some highly visible blacks who were perceived as not doing whatever they did in a way to win the applause of all their fellow blacks (*TL,* 335).

This passage is late in the book (Chapter 25: "Black Film"), which approaches a chronological order from childhood to 1980; and it serves to proceed into a calculated invective against Mason and Hollywood. The impact of this invective, in tandem with the strategy of chronological placement, is further buttressed by the fact that in the preceding chapters Poitier fashions himself in such a manner that he inveigles, to some extent, a trust and justification in his argument against Mason, bestowing even an absurdity upon Mason's comments. Poitier's quoting of "Uncle Tom," "lackey," and "house nigger," as Mason's references to him, are rendered, at the point when they are presented in his autobiography, moot and, indeed, mute (as signifiers of complicity, compliance, complacency, race treason, or effeminacy and emasculation) in light of the restoration of race and masculinity that has been performed in the preceding chapters.

The restoration of race and masculinity is through a manipulation of the private/public set of oppositions, especially ethnicity (private) and race (public).[9] Poitier's autobiography presents the reader with a narrative/developmental/geographical mapping of departure and return as a movement from community to individual back to community, from ethnic black to racially, monolithically black to racial exemplar. The departure begins in the opening Chapters 1–4 ("Cat Island," "Nassau," "Miami," and "New York," respectively). In Chapter One, Poitier tells of his family name:

The name 'Poitier' comes from Haiti. Slaves bearing that name, having made successful escapes from the Haitian plantation system, ventured into the Bahama Island areas, settling in on the first islands they encountered on their escape routes. Upon learning that the Bahama Islands consisted of seven hundred islands and cays, they set up a pattern of interisland migration that eventually brought our branch of the family to Cat Island. A generation later, my mother's branch (bearing the name 'Outten') arrived from one of the numerous plantations scattered about these British-owned islands . . . (*TL*, 6).

This reference to heritage and genealogy serves several functions: First, it positions Poitier, his family and community in the particular Caribbean and American, North and South, African diaspora. This provides an ethnic framework for understanding his early childhood and later young adult experiences as culturally different from the African Americans of Harlem, Miami, and the Hollywood acting community. Second, the reference to heritage initiates what William Boelhower (*viz.* Werner Sollars [1986]) describes as "the constitutive play between descent and consent" in the construction of the American identity: Another dichotomy, a bipolar movement in which issues of race, Old World heritage and tradition, and memory (issues of descent) are brought into a productive dynamic process of becoming self-determined, self-reliant, and independent (issues of consent) (Boelhower 1991, 130–131). The idyllic world of Cat Island is implicitly positioned in opposition to the conflicted, urbanity of Hollywood, America, and particularly the African American blackness associated with Poitier's black star persona:

> Cat Island stands out as one of the most beautiful among the thirty-five inhabited islands in the chain. It has fantastically beautiful beaches on the north side, and a 400-foot-high ridge runs almost the entire 45 miles in length, like a miniature rocky mountain, from the top of which one has an uninterrupted view of the ocean on both sides. The beaches on the north side were lined and shaded by hundreds of coconut palm trees that simply grew at random along the waterfront. Flowers, edible fruit, and berries could be found growing wild almost everywhere, thanks to ample rainfall, abundant sunshine, and rich, but precious little topsoil (*TL*, 7).

This world is later portrayed in more economic and communal terms, which implies a sense of loss in the language of narrative recounting of it:

> There was no welfare on Cat Island. Everybody worked except those who were too old or sick, and in such instances, of course, younger, healthier members of the family supported them with their labor. Older people were an integral part of the family structure, with talks appropriate to their advanced ages, until things got too difficult for them, at which time they would sit down and do nothing, assured of their continued—and revered—place in the family unit. Consequently, grandparents like mine, on my mother's side, didn't have to worry about survival when their productive years were over, since everything was

shared with them. Respect for the old ones was everywhere in evidence
in this patriarchal society. Young people were required to be honest,
live up to their responsibilities, and respect their elders (*TL*, 12).

There is an implicit other in these descriptions of life and family on Cat
Island. The description of landscape and geography performs a critique of
the urbanity of Poitier's Harlem and Hollywood self. The descriptions of
family, with "no welfare," directly refers to welfare, social programs and
dissolution of family that Poitier must encounter in his immigration to the
United States. The dynamic of descent and consent early in the narrative
initiates a critical hermeneutic device from which the present star figure is
presented as a figure of transformation.

The figural movement of the private self (the island self) to the public
self (black star persona) is doubly signified as a figure of transformation
when one considers notions of gender that are presented and critiqued in
these opening chapters. The most critical commentaries on Sidney Poitier's
star image were that he was asexual and his characters often isolated from
the black community and, therefore, non-threatening to the established cultural imagery of whiteness. The image was not a threat to masculinity or the
social barriers of race, which his characters seemingly challenged (see Bogle
1988; Boyd 1997; George 1994; and Guerrero 1993). Indeed, Poitier's screen
image was saintly, overly dignified, and within the confines of the social
problem film[10], Poitier's image was overdetermined by the narrative and
generic use of race (the "problem") and the overcoming of race as a coming
to consciousness of whiteness: Poitier's image was the consciousness of the
nation. However, the movement between ethnic and racial (which parallels
the movement between descent and consent) mediates a dialog between the
public image of Poitier's masculinity—the critical commentary on it—and the
private man. This dialog on gender is more confessional, establishing the first
chapter as a recounting of a passage into manhood and loss of innocence.
Episodic vignettes provide a frank discussion of his childhood sexuality (the
fluidity and aggressiveness of which counters his asexual, docile screen
image), recounting his adventures in the wilds of the island, culminating in
his father sending him away (to Miami and the control of an older brother)
because of his quickly burgeoning manhood (*TL*, 9–16).

Later in Chapters Two and Three ("Nassau" and "Miami," respectively), the critical, confessional engagement with the acquisition of masculinity, via adventure, sexuality and rites of passage into manhood are
allegorically re-configured in the motions of migration and immigration. In
the early discussions of his family's migration from Cat Island to the urban
island of Nassau, at the young age of ten, Poitier is full of awe and wonder:

> We sailed all that evening and into the next day, until someone called out, 'There's Nassau.' [ . . . ] Suddenly I could make out objects in motion, scurrying about at great speed. I asked my mother what they were and she said they were cars. I had never seen a car before, and as we drew nearer to the island these beetlelike fellows absorbed my complete attention. With eyes wide and mouth dropped open, I stepped ashore into this fascinating new place, this big city with people—cars—electricity—and other strange things I had never seen before (*TL*, 18–19).

From this moment of movement and wonder, Poitier narrates his loss of virginity, the development of his "hustling" skills, and his burgeoning criminal skills. Consequently, four years later, with the street name of Sidney "P," Poitier had become a young urban denizen, complete with the hazards and potential long-term problems of urban youth and his father's admittance to his loss of control over his son. After stealing corn and having to see a judge about the possible legal consequences, Poitier recounts his father's decision to send him to Miami and his own fear of himself and his situation:

> The next day I was taken to the chambers of the judge, where my father had to pay for the corn, again with borrowed money. On the way home, he said to me, 'You know, boy, I can't run after you anymore. I'm getting on in years and you seem determined to get into trouble . . . you were born in the United States and we want you to go back there. You will have a chance to go to school and try to make something of yourself . . . '. There I was still dancing close to the flames, with the stakes getting higher and higher. Playful mischief by now had escalated to petty larceny. From Cat Island, where theft was practically unknown, to this place where it came close to being a survival tool. Yes, sir, Nassau was different from Cat Island, and the nature of the daring chances I had grown used to taking was a reflection of that difference. I had a devil-may-care attitude, while at the same time I was scared of what the devil might decide to lay on me. I knew if I got caught at some of my devil-may-care stunts, I was gone—four years gone (*TL*, 29).

I have gone through these rather lengthy excerpts from the first two chapters in order to demonstrate that, first, Poitier places an emphasis on the acquisition of masculinity as movement, as a passage, but also as a certain loss of innocence and as a threat of loss (for the "four years gone" is a reference to the potential for reform school and to the actual loss of a friend to the reform school system [*TL*, 28–29]); second, the emphasis on acquisition, ambiguity and loss directs the reader to the instability, and learned management of that instability, in masculinity.

Furthermore, the double signification of movement as migration and acquisition is seen in the performative attainment of African American blackness. Though in his move to Miami Poitier does not legally immigrate (because of his status as an American citizen), his upbringing on Cat Island and in Nassau allows for a distinctly different understanding and confrontation to race. Once in Miami with his older brother, sister-in-law, and family, Poitier experiences cultural differences which are first linked to lifestyle, country/city distinction and then to notions of race and cultural blackness; there is an estrangement, a defamiliarization of blackness in language and cultural value:

> Instantly upon meeting my sister-in-law and my nieces and nephews, I realized I was in an entirely new set of social and cultural circumstances. I didn't understand these people—and they didn't understand me. I had come from a place seemingly as far away as Mars; they had heard about the Bahamas, but most of them had never been there. It was a strange time for me. I spoke with a different accent from theirs. I know nothing of the kind of life they lived, and because their values were quite foreign tome, naturally communication was difficult. [ . . . ] In fact, it was so traumatic, that whole experience, that I was never able to adjust to Miami (*TL*, 41).

And there is also the confrontation with the "fact of blackness" in the American context. In his recounting of his experience as a pharmacy delivery boy being asked to use the backdoor, Poitier records a sense of astonishment at this treatment:

> [When asked to go around to the backdoor] It was easy enough from my point of view, for her to just take the package. She slammed the door in my face and I put the package down on the doorstep and I left. I wasn't accustomed to such behavior on the part of ladies, white or black, and having been reared in an area where I never ran into that kind of thing, I was definitely not about to accommodate myself to it in this strange new place. Furthermore, while admittedly I was not completely naïve about racial matters, I was certainly not afraid of white people (*TL*, 42).

The outcome of this experience, and the later encounter with the Klan, leads Poitier to view blackness critically in respect to whiteness, allowing for distanciation of self from external images. In a moment of observation at his own behavior, Poitier considers his predicament as one of self-image: "Possibly because I didn't know any better at that time, which was due in part to my spending the first fifteen years of my life free of the crushing negative self-image hammered into black children by this system, in this Miami, in this America" (*TL*, 42–43).

Poitier's cultural position, his relation to American blackness as outsider, as immigrant, as ethnic black in relation to his family and the Miami (and by extension American) community initiates a narrative of cultural assimilation and integration into American society, a narrative of racial consciousness, a consciousness of the self which is at odds with societal notions of race. Poitier recounts meticulously and frankly the loss of his Caribbean accent, his self-education, his individual success and failure as a restaurant owner, and his overall achievement of the "American dream" with his success as an actor. Yet, throughout his narrative self-presentation, Poitier maintains a critical insight into the question of race and blackness, an insight which is linked to an internal dialog between the struggles of black manhood and masculinity in America and the honor and responsibility of manhood instilled in him by his father and in his Caribbean upbringing.

The Americanization of the self is tempered by a particular formation of blackness, one which is directed at the struggles—social and political, as well as representational—of the black man as blackness and black men are constructed in the American society: monolithic, emasculated, pathological and in constant battle against these constructions. What emerges in the private narrative development of masculinity and blackness is what Hazel Carby (1999) has called the Race Man, a public figure of both gender and race. For the Race Man there is an imagined black community whose future (social, political, and intellectual) is determined by gender and a "struggle among men over the bodies of women" (Carby 25). The figure of the Race Man is also informed by DuBois, Carby's paramount figure of the Race Man, and his notion of the Talented Tenth (" . . . Leaders of thought and missionaries of culture among their people . . ."), a model of exceptionalism and uplift. The aforementioned development of Poitier's racial consciousness is simultaneously a development of a gender consciousness.

There are two specific sites in the development of the gender/race conscious Race Man in *This Life*. First, gender (anxiety and the failure of gender responsibility) and race responsibility figure in Poitier's discussion of "tensions" in his first marriage. In Chapter 13 ("Tensions"), Poitier is an exemplar and a figure of patriarchal masculinity, the breadwinner, the father figure, the husband; it is an image quite to the contrary of popular notions of black masculinity. Furthermore, it is an image in conflict, in turmoil, in crisis, brought about by the burden of responsibility during his first comments about his marriage and in opposition to the "kind of woman" his wife, Juanita, had become during their marriage:

> Tensions in the marriage were surfacing more frequently by the middle of 1957. I was more likely to roam around than not. I began to grow resentful that I was growing in one direction and Juanita in another (*TL*, 197).

And still further:

> My wife just didn't understand enough of what was going on inside me to help—perhaps I hadn't been able to open myself up to her. I believe the only person who might have understood the kind of pressure that could build up in a young man locked into rat-racing in New York, who twelve or thirteen years before was walking around the sandy beaches of the Caribbean with not a thought in his head (*TL*, 198).

Masculinity, indeed, becomes a mysterious, indecipherable "thing." "Tensions" becomes a pivotal chapter in that it chronicles not only the crisis of masculinity, as loss of freedom and as a burden of responsibility, but also links the resolution of this crisis to the development of a responsibility to race and black manhood:

> I was somehow being pushed to save the world. I was somehow being pushed to raise my black brothers and sisters to the next level. I was being pushed to change the world as it related to me and mine. I was being pushed to do the impossible. I figured that black people just wouldn't survive without me saving them through dealing with the pressures on myself. I didn't think the *world* would survive if I didn't live and develop in a certain way (*TL*, 198).

The projection of the crisis of race and masculinity is further elaborated in the commitment to responsibility to his family and the threat to his family caused by his affair with Diahann Carroll. In Chapter 16 ("Diahann"), Poitier recounts the beginning of his affair with Carroll and raises ethical questions as gender questions and questions of responsibility the family and to the wife. There is a re-articulation of exemplary behavior through his re-statement of his father's words about family and fatherhood as his own motivating dilemma:

> Those words [the words of advice from his father][11] began to waken in
> me on that morning when I told my wife I was involved with another
> woman, and they came surging up with a vengeance that evening to
> jam my thoughts whenever the possibility of leaving my children was
> verbalized, creating what was to become in time a conflict of such pro-
> portions that I can hardly describe it (*TL*, 231).

Through the use of autobiography Poitier is an exemplar with the ethical
dilemma of fidelity in the marriage. However, this problem is gendered, is a
"man's take," so to speak, because of the way in which the wife, her incompleteness, becomes the problem; and she becomes a problem because she is
*only* a wife, which is not enough for the man, to the exemplary figure of
race and masculinity that he has become. His wife, Juanita, therefore, falls
short, is to blame:

> Fostering a resentment through all these years and not being able to
> communicate with Juanita or she with me, except on the most elemen-
> tal level, I instantly became angry at the slightest reminder that she was
> quite content while my needs were going begging. Why couldn't she
> develop a meaningful interest in my work so I could have someone with
> whom I could intelligently discuss all my never-ending problems? Why
> were so many of my most vulnerable moments endured without a reas-
> suring touch? Admittedly, among my needs were some even I could not
> articulate and which Juanita would be at a dead loss simply trying to
> understand, much less serve (*TL*, 231).

The construction of himself as a victim, here and in the next chapter, serves
to vilify femininity:

> I was still living by trail and error—by instinct. I was living by a body
> of reactive mechanisms I had accumulated in my strange, overcrowded
> existence. There I was in my thirties and had been through several life-
> times already. And I was in a mess—a real mess. On the one hand I had
> found a woman who was in tune with my needs, a woman who I
> believed would satisfy both my mind and my body [Diahann Carrol].
> On the other hand, I was married and had children who my father said
> I must protect and never leave (*TL*, 232).

Coming to consciousness of gender and race, consequently, is an overcoming and transcending of a prior self. This is an almost typical story.

However, it is in next chapter (Chapter 17: "A Raisin in the Sun") where we find the second site of the simultaneity of gender and race consciousness. Here Poitier works to raise questions about the construct of black masculinity. He does so by constructing the "black masculine problem" as the problem of a victim, which is in and of itself the nature of the construction of a problem:

> I believed from the first day I went into rehearsal that the play should not unfold from the mother's point of view. I still believe that. I think for maximum effect, *A Raisin in the Sun* should unfold from the point of view of the son, . . . (*TL,* 234).

His explanation is that to have the play emphasize the mother would detract from the problems of the black man, but before that:

> They accused me of 'star' behavior. Of wanting to be the top dog on stage. The simple truth of the matter was that if the play is told from the point of view of the mother, and you don't have an actor playing the part of Walter Lee strongly, then the end result may very well be a negative comment on the black male. . . . They professed to be at a loss as to the underlying reason for my feeling about the image of the black male. But I was in the dark every bit as much as they were . . . (*TL,* 235).
>
> He [the character "Walter Lee"] could appear as a weak man overwhelmed by his mother—incapable of engineering his own life, which he has based on dreams that exceed his skills; in other words, a weakling who doesn't deserve very much attention. Or he could appear as the average man with an average potential and average dreams, who fails to achieve them only through a combination of misunderstandings in his own family and the racism of his environment—a man who winds up bested not because he is incapable but because circumstances conspire against him—a far cry from a weakling who is reaching beyond his grasp (*TL,* 236).

The image of the "black man" becomes paramount in the portrayal of the black family: the battle over the character of "Walter Lee," the need to relocate the signification of race and the critique of race relations in the play is now re-thematized by Poitier within the notion of black manhood as the responsible expression of race and family/community. It is no wonder that when Poitier recounts the reception of the Academy Award for Best Actor in *Lilies the Field* that there is the pronominal shift from "I" to "we" and the autobiographical movement of voice from the individual to the community: Poitier has fully confirmed his status as a Race Man by speaking for the race: "We black people had done it. We were capable. We forget sometimes, having to persevere against unspeakable odds, that we are capable of infinitely more than the culture is yet willing to credit to our account" (*TL*, 255).

It is through these processes of racialization and gendering, of becoming an African American man, a model and spokesman, both exceptional and ordinary, that Poitier is charged with the responsibility of racial representation and uplift. Furthermore, through his expressed privacy (as a public figure), performance style and characters performed, and through his presentation of the self, Poitier embodies a solidly middle class model of black manhood. His stylings of race and class offer his viewing and reading public a process of masculine attainment which incorporates class moral and ethical values as racial and gender values.

Let me summarize the discussion thus far: By following the developmental narrative of Poitier's autobiography, I have tried to demonstrate, first, that as a star text Poitier articulates personhood through a discourse of individuality, signifying possibility, the possibility of the average individual to succeed. Second, Poitier's personhood is also a negotiation of the ethnic *versus* racial self as the ethnic black confronts African American cultural blackness. In this instance, Poitier maps, through migration and immigration, his assimilation into African American blackness. Moreover, the consent to blackness is demonstrated through the rescue and acquisition of the trope of black manhood from the loss of family and masculine responsibility. On the one hand, Poitier's autobiography itself as a star text posits these developments as exemplary, as a model of race and gender. On the other hand, the ascent to Race Man posits an ethico-political incompleteness which in the gesture of self-presentation in the autobiographical form is a process of authentication. *This Life* provides a catalog of Poitier's coming to gender and racial consciousness and provides the space for him to offer authenticating "facts" and gestures of his commitment to the black community.

To return to the opening comments about "Black Films" and Poitier: the gathered racial, ethnic, and masculine self that Poitier presents through the developmental narrative strategy allows for the textual confrontation between Mason's critique and Poitier's star persona to be configured as a confrontation about commitment, authenticity and cultural authority. For as a Race Man, Poitier's status as spokesman is predicated upon his "proof" of blackness, his commitment to community, the authenticity of his "black experience" and his black masculinity—all of which he has demonstrated through the telling of his story and all of which serve to strengthen and authorize his critique of Hollywood and his own self-critique of his function in Hollywood as counter-critique to his critics:

> What I resented most about Clifford Mason by the time of our second encounter was his laying of all the film industry's transgressions at my feet. [ . . . ] I respected the rage and hostility of my fellow actors against the unfairness that, first, kept them out so long and, second, when the door did begin to open, showered so many opportunities on one person, in the tokenism that my presence was. [ . . . ] But I stood ready to fight Clifford Mason's or anyone else's attempt to charge me with even a fraction more [mistakes] than in my opinion I deserved.
>
> Hollywood had not kept it a secret that it wasn't interested in supplying blacks with a variety of positive images. In fact, in only a few isolated corners of the industry could one find committed souls who could be classified as interested in supplying blacks with a different image from what they had been accustomed to. Thanks to that handful of committed souls, the image of the black man just scratching his head was changing. A black man was put in a suit with a tie, given a briefcase; he could become a doctor, a lawyer, or a police detective. That was a plus factor for us, to be sure, but it certainly was not enough to satisfy the yearnings of an entire people. It simply wasn't. Because a people are a community, and a community consists of bus drivers and laborers and street sweepers and dentists and schoolteachers and hustlers and prostitutes and students and ordinary workers—people, people. They fall in love, they have problems, they have children, they live, they die. Where was that kind of representation on the motion picture screen for blacks? It didn't exist. The closest Hollywood came over a twelve-year period was the one-dimensional, middle-class imagery I embodied most of the time. Although I and a handful of friends in those isolated corners "inside" Hollywood considered it a step forward, it was not a step that could in any way alleviate all the frustrations of the past decades. I understood the value system of a make-believe town that was at its heart a racist place (*TL*, 337–338).

Though these comments mark a strong critique of Hollywood, they also signal, even within his own autobiography, the end of the star persona, Sidney Poitier. At this juncture Poitier becomes the cultural critic, focusing his comments on film, the function of film, and the responsibility of the artist. Within the trajectory of his public image and career, the shift is marked by an increased presence behind the camera in production and directing.

His fall from grace, as it were, was a sign of the times. Poitier, as a film star, cultural producer, and Race Man, was suspended in a web of representation which extended in debate across the two domains of simulacral realism and mimetic realism. Drawing on Baudrillard, Harper (1996) describes television programming and televisual aesthetics, where they portrayed African Americans, as simulacral realism, as "propounding scenarios that might subsequently (or consequently) be realized through out the larger social field, regardless of whether they actually pre-exist there," against the demands for mimetic realism, which would properly " 'reflect' the social reality on which it was implicitly modeled" (160).[12] Though Harper makes this aesthetic difference in reference to television shows of the late 60s and early 70s (shows like *Julia, I Spy, The Leslie Uggams Show*), the same distinction can be made in reference to Poitier's social problem films and the ensuing criticisms against them. In films like those of his 1967 reign (*Guess Who's Coming to Dinner, In the Heat of the Night, To Sir with Love*), the germane issues of racism, integration, and interracial marriage raise the question of realism as one of Poitier's characters' failure to re-present everyday African Americans, thereby, in that failure, representing an inauthentic black experience and unrealistic societal race relations. The films re-present progressive, integrationist scenarios as representations of already existing realities, realities which, criticism argued, were unrealized in the social world outside of the films.

Poitier's characters were, indeed, visions of black men and blackness not realized, or not yet realized on the scale imagined in the films at that time: His characters were ironic figures of integration: Singular, high-ranking doctor/administrator, marrying a white woman; a northern, black detective in the South, waiting for a train; and a black school teacher bringing order to white hoodlums: Figures of an outsider integrated into or integrating white communities, while simultaneously removed and isolated from the filmic black community. Furthermore, his performances were linguistically isolated from the vernacular performances of the few black characters in his films, and particularly, in *Guess* and *In the Heat,* Poitier's characters are an economic class removed from the few members of the black filmic black community.[13]

The ironic moment of the integrated black man, on the one hand, can be understood within the notion of entertainment, offering utopian fantasies of integration. However, on the other hand, as the core divergence of the aesthetics of simulacral and mimetic realism suggest, and as the then contemporary criticism of Poitier and television further suggests, the debate about Poitier is about authentic versus inauthentic blackness. This core debate has overlapping discursive oppositional sets, such as vernacular *versus* middle class; black arts *versus* American pop cultural forms of blackness; and separation *versus* integration, roughly corresponding to the authentic versus inauthentic.[14] In further examination of these debates and the rise of the black athlete as actor and Blaxploitation, the oppositions in the authentic/inauthentic debate are also debates about masculine difference.

To begin with Sidney Poitier is to begin with a singular figure of the black masculine in American popular film culture. Prior to Poitier the catalog of imagery for black men in film, as outlined by Bogle (1973), was that of toms, coon, and bucks. These images were in the service of the perpetuation of the myth of whiteness, as one of humanity, civility and superiority. Though hasty in his categorization, Bogle's schema does have the advantage of tracing this image history from *Birth of a Nation* to the Blaxploitation era of the '70s, an image history which is fairly accurate except where it concerns Poitier. As Cripps (1977 and 1993) notes, Poitier's image emerged out of turmoil in the film industry. Cripps notes the change in the industry and in the image to the post-World War II national consciousness was in part due to the political actions of the National Association for the Advancement of Colored People (NAACP) across the national front and specifically in Hollywood, where the organization called for a change in the kind of imagery produced. The social problem film soon emerged as the genre of film which most allowed for the re-configuration of race and its associates, gender and class. Films like *Home of the Brave* (dealing with the black veteran), *Pinky* and *Lost Boundaries* (dealing with passing) and *Intruder in the Dust* (the screen adaptation of Faulkner's novel by the same name, dealing with Southern racism and lynch mob mentalities) appear in 1949, marking a dramatically different discourse of race than preceding generations. Race in these films was a sign of human consciousness, though quite problematically: As the narrator comments about Lucas Beauchamp (Juano Hernandez) in the end of *Intruder in the Dust*, Beauchamp, his dignity and suffering through the false accusation of race, of being black, is the "conscience of us all."

Indeed, by the 1950s, race in American film had become the site of redemption for whiteness. It is from this conflicted site of noble savagery, redemption and race-serving humanism that Poitier emerges to become the most significant black star of post-WW II American film.[15] Poitier's characters were noble figures of masculine dignity, but again, not without problems. Poitier's characters were often counter to the toms and coons tradition in that they were doctors, teachers, ordinary workers, or rebellious youth or race conscious clergymen or the black detective. However, Poitier's character were always "saint like" in that their constructions as characters isolated them from the filmic black community or their inordinate amount of human sacrifice rendered them a series of long suffering nobles in the service of the salvation of the white characters. His characters were once removed from the privilege of whiteness, only serving, in the long run, to buttress whiteness, and especially white masculinity, as a signifier of humanity and ethical subjectivity. In other words, Poitier's characters had indeed achieved a status, an ethical and categorical status, above the shuffling and jiving of Tomdom residing black men; however, Poitier's black men were merely a stage, of sorts, in the attainment of ethical and just masculinity of white characters. Yet, Poitier and his characters are not without achievement in their historical context and certainly worthy of re-evaluation in light of the overall project here.

For Cripps (1993), Poitier's integrationist image had been an instrument, along with the social problem film genre, promoting the film industry's liberal ideals; and his usefulness promoting these ideals, as the public response to him suggested, had exhausted itself (284–294). Ed Guerrero (1993) similarly notes that the social problem film formula offered little relevance to the changing cultural climate; and, therefore, neither did Poitier. Guerrero further links Poitier's downfall to the rise in consciousness as seen in the Black Arts Movement and the release of *Sweet Sweetback's Baad Asssss Song* (Melvin Van Peebles 1971).

However, as I have tried to suggest, the Poitier project was part of a larger plan. To return to Poitier's self-restoration and the autobiography: Through the use of autobiography as a technique of the self and self-fashioning, Poitier posits himself as an exemplar and as ethically incomplete. In doing so, Poitier establishes himself as a Race Man, an ascent to a racialized "boy," a re-articulation of the "boy" in this chapter's title. In racializing the category of boy, Poitier foregrounds the construction of race and gender in class, ethnicity and social and civil ideals of democracy.

Chapter Three

# Super Bad: Jim Brown, Blaxploitation and the Coming of Boyz

The emphasis of this chapter is masculine difference. In understanding masculine difference, I rely on Eve K. Sedgwick's (1985) notion of homosociality and the resulting economy of masculinity in which there are gendered relationships within masculinity: "[Homosocial] is a word occasionally used in history and the social sciences, where it describes social bonds between persons of the same sex; it is a neologism, obviously formed by analogy with 'homosexual,' and just as obviously meant to be distinguished from 'homosexual.' . . . [I]t is applied to such activities as 'male bonding,' . . ." (1). Sedgwick continues to return the homosocial to the "orbit of desire"; however, for the purpose here, an understanding of homosociality and the homosocial as a hegemonically gendering enterprise displaces homosocial desire. By this I mean that homosociality provides a spectrum of gendered relations within masculinity. This spectrum is considered hegemonic in that the homosocial—its ruptures and permutations and its inclusions and exclusions—serve to incorporate non-ideal masculinities into a range of the "permissible," ordering a universe of gender relations in which masculinity is the dominate and dominating form of gender. Furthermore, I configure the space of the homosocial as the space of the historical and intertextual exchange between and among images of men and masculinity. I emphasize masculine difference as it is signified by body type, class, and race.

The path I follow is again winding and discontinuous, taking as my object not only masculinity, but also femininity as the most prominent site of certain debates around class and the black community. The focus of the chapter lies, however, in two areas: first, I examine Jim Brown's crossover and the introduction of the black "macho"; the relationship between the black macho and Poitier's class-ed, saint image; and both Poitier and Brown's incorporation into ideal masculinity and whiteness. Second, I examine how the masculine types of Blaxploitation, in the symbolic exploitation of popular black culture, precipitates a debate in the black public sphere around class and masculine difference which informs the category of boyz.

## JIM BROWN AND WARRIOR CROSSOVER

Before beginning the discussion of Jim Brown, an elaboration of "crossover" is necessary. The notion of crossover is informed by and negotiated from the music industrial notion of "going mainstream," moving from one market audience to another (Garofalo 1990); it is also informed by star studies (Britton 1991; and Dyer 1979 and 1986). What emerges is a notion of movement from one audience to another through genre and image. Implicit in the radio model of crossover (when considering black musical artists) is the entrance into and development of a mainstream audience (i.e., getting a song on an album oriented radio [AOR] station playlist), and implicit in the notion of "mainstream" is a racialized market, predominantly white, suburban and middle class. With film, on the other hand, there are two differences which slightly modify the notion of crossover.

First, as a mode of storytelling, film deploys characterization; consequently, the actor/actress (as analogous to the singer) is performing a character, which in turn deploys the body, as a signifier, quite differently than in music. In other words, the performance of a character, particularly in Hollywood film and "fact" based films, is often congruent with the notion of the "race" of the actor or actress, whereas in music the song is not necessarily a signifier of "race" in that style and mimicry can often signify appropriation or commodification of "race" (e.g., "blue-eyed soul"). In addition, with music and song, the disembodied voice is the narrative mode, with the body as an instrument or vessel. In other words, the song carries the story, not necessarily through the body of the singer as much as through the delivery of the song. Consequently, there is more fluidity in who performs the song, as opposed to who performs the character.

Second, the visuality of the text creates a certain stasis in which body and voice become entangled in the performative visual codes of race and gender. In film, for example, the racialized body is always that, a racialized body, which is attached to the voice as a signifier of something else which contradicts or confirms race. The stasis of the visual body is further complicated by notions of genre in which the body, through iconicity and costume, is coded in very particular ways and in which the star, as character, is generically determined within narrative. The filmic model of crossover, then, implies the movement from one genre to another with the vocal and corporeal residues (as these residues are determined by race and body) of another genre remaining attached to the visual image of the star.

The understanding of crossover as movement and corporeality is important in understanding the screen persona of Jim Brown and his movement from the athletic to the filmic and the implication of his body as a type of body. As an athlete, Jim Brown already had an audience pre-formed by a spectacular college and professional football career. In his film career, what crosses over is not only his audience, but also a spirit of athleticism and an acceptance of this athleticism as a sign of racial progress and universal success. Witness an early biographer's description of Brown as a black superman:

> It was Jim brown who, during the decade from 1957 to 1965, had done more than any other man to originate what became a national obsession with the game. He was a consistent and spectacular warrior, the embodiment of his team, a crystallization of physical potency. More, he introduced a new dimension to the sport, as its first black hero.
>
> [ . . . ] He had invaded the American imagination, black and white, with a thrust only rare figures in a generation achieve. When he shifted gears and became, in less than a year, a movie star, the potential of his influence erased limitation. If there were a black boy anywhere in America whose vision of manhood excluded both sports and entertainment, he was a freak, a mutation of consciousness. Apart from serving as channels of style for stored rage, such endeavors provided the cleanest entrance into the American dream of independence, power, wealth and fame, the promise almost exclusively of whites before the sixties. . . . His form of life, relation to both races, feelings about America, satisfaction or frustration with his own role, would suggest much about the nature of the dream, whether it was worth pursuing or whether . . . its achievement, . . . , solved no significant problems and, at best, compounded original dilemmas.
>
> So by coming to know Brown and, . . . , by writing about him, one could hope to approach and to understand certain mysteries in America as well as measure one of her largest and darkest heroes (Toback 1971, 6–7).

In this rather lengthy description, Brown's body is configured as a well-oiled machine that "thrusts" into action, whose "gears" easily "shift," propelling the body/machine from one domain of spectacle to the next.

Also for James Toback (who later directed Brown in *Fingers* [1978]), the body/machine is a sign of the American ingenuity of self-invention, allowing Brown's success is be translated into a paragon of the American Dream which, in the sheer power of Brown's athleticism, transcends class and racial boundaries. Through his incorporation into Toback's notion of the American Dream, Brown becomes the site of understanding, self-awareness and masculine redemption for Toback himself. Furthermore, at the same time that Toback celebrates the spectacular transcendence of Brown's masculine prowess, Brown's masculinity itself becomes *a* masculinity, a form of black manhood, counter to the "freak, mutation of consciousness," that is the black boy who does not participate in sports or entertainment. Brown is simultaneously the American Dream and the model for the entrance into consciousness of masculinity.

Brown's incorporation into ideal American masculinity is re-duplicated in the space and economy of filmic masculinity with his arrival as a film star. However, what is noteworthy of this incorporation is Brown's relation to other filmic black masculinities. Brown is visually marked by his athletic body, which, in turn, in the homosocial becomes a sign of masculine difference. Indeed, in the *Ebony* article (October 1969), "Football Heroes Invade Hollywood," it is the athletic body which is foregrounded in the notion of crossover from football to film screen:

> Straight out of American legend and mythology a new brand of Hollywood screen character is emerging: the black superman. Whether he is hero, antihero or hero's foil, he stands tall and muscular, exudes overstated masculinity and is usually accustomed to trotting his rugged good looks around a football field . . . (195).

The article catalogues the then recent emergence of the black athlete as the black actor, commenting on Jim Brown, Fred Williamson, Rosie Grier, O.J. Simpson, and the earlier Paul Robeson and Woody Strode, among others. However, comments on the body, stature, height, and strength are the driving force of the article ("handsome faces;" "muscular bodies;" "beautifully muscled gladiator;" "he-man physique"). In this case, as with Toback, there is the athletic body as the American dream of success and achievement. However, within the class and race discourse of *Ebony,* the emphasis on the physique of the black superman directs the reader to three conflicting points: first, the author is deliberately placing black athletes, as race-ed bodies, indeed as black athletes and supermen, into the pantheon of the aesthetics of athletics, of the athletic masculine body form as the universal ideal of humanity, as the ideal of the human form[1]; second, "straight out of

American legend and mythology" suggests that the black athlete has an organic, integrationist presence and history as a popular hero, and as an athlete, expressing masculinity, team work and discipline—despite race—, the black athlete is a transcendent figure, moving beyond race, emphasizing one's physical ability to succeed; and third, though more implicit, as the race-ed body, the black athlete ("gladiator" and "he-man") is also the sexualized body, the object of spectatorial desire.[2] The author of the article does appear to be aware of these conflicting points, as are seen in the comments on the emergence of the black athletes in film as a "deep and shallow change," but the author seems to be unaware of the emergence of this image as counter to the other image then present, that of Sidney Poitier.

The most prominent and profitable former football player working at the time was Jim Brown, and as Guerrero (1993) notes in reference to *100 Rifles* (Tom Gries, 1969): " . . . Brown was able to do what Poitier was denied in his career to that point, to act in a violent assertive manner and express his sexuality openly and beyond dominant cinema's sexual taboo" (79). The muscular, brute, athletic body was counter to the slim, clothed, middle-class body as the sexual to the asexual (or at most implied sexual). Guerrero continues to note that Brown's characters were part of "a coordinated team, the integrationist paradigm" (in films like *The Dirty Dozen*). "Integration" and "integrationist" were the same paradigms and discursive mediators of Poitier's image as well; however, Poitier remained at the edge of sexual expression. Poitier's characters were never able to be sexual while a tool for the integrationist social problem film, yet—within the integrationist narratives of the war film (teamwork) and the western (conquest)—Jim Brown was. Part of the divergence in the integrationist models of black masculinity lies in the "types" and star personae that were Sidney Poitier and Jim Brown (Bogle 1988 and Guerrero 1993). As Guerrero notes: "Offscreen Poitier was reserved and well mannered, thus sticking closely to his screen persona; Jim Brown was a turbulent personality who entangled himself in offscreen escapades, fist fights and rancorous feuds on and off set" (79).

The images of Poitier and Brown instantiate an economy of filmic black masculinity. In her discussions of late eighteenth century and nineteenth century French male nude painting, Abigail Solomon-Godeau (1997) establishes an economy of masculine imagery which is useful in the discussion of Poitier and Brown. Solomon-Godeau discusses masculine imagery and the legacy of the male nude as one of masculine differences. The polls of the manly warrior body type, muscular and athletic, and the ephebe body type, lean and sinewy, serve to broaden and incorporate masculine difference, different kinds of masculinity, within the realm of ideal masculinity. In considering the legacy of the male nude, the importance of the black *beau idèals* is how the racially inflected masculine ephebe and warrior enter into the existing economy of whiteness. On the surface Brown and Poitier are contemporary racialized versions, transcodings of the extreme polls of *beau idèals:* Brown the virile, muscular warrior type and Poitier the elegant, graceful ephebe: both masculine types, the divergence between them being signs of masculine difference.

As the well-educated and mannered black man who is often paired as buddy to a white character and whose presence motivates the morality of the narrative, Poitier embodies the American democratic ethos and the "black as the ethical principle" (Wiegman 1991; and Appiah 1993, respectively).[3] In both embodiments the black male is assumed masculine and a representation of "good." The difference lies in the use of blackness as a configuration of the democratic ethos and the ethical principle. In both blackness is a marking, a coding which determines blackness, dark skin and phenomenal difference from whiteness, as a natural signifier of cultural conventions and politics (Snead 1994, 5). The embodiment of the American ethos, which is contingent upon the interracial buddy relation and its recuperative potential, operates as a commodity exchange (an exchange between gendered, yet oppositely racially codified bodies) in the construction of a whole ideal (through the visual salvation and celebration of the white male body). The figure of the Saint, the embodiment of the ethical principle, is less dependent upon the racially opposingly paired buddies, as it is upon the legacy of Poitier's characters as singular figures of blackness, as metaphorical figures in which contemporary politics and significations of blackness and racial justice are over determinedly invested. The saint-like qualities of Poitier's characters promote suffering and moral vindication. Poitier's masculinity, as a masculine gender image, hinges upon the tropological transformations of racialized masculinity (the black man) into a figure of honor, dignity, and sacrifice: Black masculinity and the battle for recognition and respect is a trial, a redemptive struggle to find and overcome the shortcomings and failings of whiteness. This transformation of blackness to ethical and figurative device re-positions and absorbs black men in an economy of imagery, an economy of white masculinity (particularly in reference to the social problem film, where Poitier's characters are figures of inclusion and integration).

As an athlete, the virtue of manhood, and the virtuosity of Brown's masculinity, exceeds race, allowing Brown to enter laterally, into a seemingly egalitarian celebration of the masculine ideal. Jim Brown's masculine gender image tropes race and masculinity as signs of brutality and aggression: Black masculinity is marked as masculine within the gendered notion of sexual aggression and the racialized notion of brutality. In other words, Brown becomes the black masculine as hypersexual; however, again, in a film like *100 Rifles,* where there is an interracial sex scene, this sexuality is permissible (as opposed to Poitier).[4] Whereas the fear of sexuality and sexual expression is contained in class, effeminacy, and morality in the image of Poitier as sexual passivity, it is the hypersexualized, black masculine which is inserted into the economy of masculinity as a sports figure, as a man who has a function in a group or team, as part of a functioning unit. The black athlete turned actor is integrated into filmic masculinity as a sexual unit, expressing a sexuality which is incorporated into whiteness as masculine difference; the difference of race is disavowed, denied as racial difference and integrated into the spectrum of masculinity and the economy of filmic masculinity. Brown's sexuality is permissible on these grounds, as a surrogate masculine, sexual being (Gooding-Williams 1995).

Poitier's characters are integrated, yet within the purview of masculine possibility. Indeed, as an ethical principle, the blackness and masculinity Poitier embodies must remain as a thing to be lost and recuperated as possibility, as something possible, even utopian. Brown, on the other hand, is a cathartic sexual image integrating blackness into whiteness, performing an imaginary reconciliation within whiteness, allowing it, through masculine difference, to reconcile and *re*-present (and represent) its animal, sexual and aggressive self.

One can argue, as does Bogle (1973 and 1988), that the ephebe, asexual and conciliatory Poitier image and the warrior type, sexual and assimilatory Brown image are rearticulations of the Tom and the Brute, respectively; however, this deferral to stereotypes ignores the use of these figures of black masculinity as incorporations into the dominate type of whiteness and white masculinity. In other words, the figures of the Tom and Brute are constructions of whiteness, *viz.* the invisibility of whiteness, *viz.* the visibility of whiteness as a signifier of the norm, of "everyman," without the divestiture of whiteness as a signifier of racial superiority.

## BLAXPLOITATION AND MASCULINE DIFFERENCE

However, whiteness and integration were not the only mediators of masculine difference broadening the possibilities of black filmic masculinity. As black film and cultural historians have noted, the divergent imagery between Poitier and Brown, the stars and character types, was part of a concerted effort at developing markets, increasing box office returns and conceding to social and political protest and unrest.[5] Guerrero best summarizes the industrial, social and political influences which led finally to the demise of Poitier as the singular black star and to the loss of Brown to the redundancy of Blaxploitation:

Only when Hollywood found itself confronted with the familiar, menacing conjunction of multiple political economic forces did it begin to act. This was, again, to be true from 1968–1972, as mounting political pressure combined with the film industry's threatened economic position. Thus political economic conditions, along with the allure and profitability of a rising black box office, proved irresistible. In 1971, with the megahit success of the independent Melvin Van Peebles's *Sweet Sweetback's BaadassssSong*, followed within a few months by Gordon Parks's nearly as successful mainstream hit *Shaft*, the Blaxploitation boom took off, and Hollywood's formula for the 'new' filmic representation of black began to crystallize (85–86).

Van Peebles' *Sweet Sweetback* and Gordon Parks's *Shaft,* and to a lesser extent Gordon Parks, Jr.'s *Superfly,* alerted the film industry to the viability of industry based "black films" and the market of the black audience. The success of the independently produced *Sweetback* and the industry produced *Shaft* mark the beginning of the Blaxploitation era.

Blaxploitation is credited with introducing the "bad nigger" type to the array of filmic black masculinity (Guerrero 86). As a type, the bad nigger challenges the established organizations and paradigms of whiteness as a figure of blackness and masculinity which cannot be integrated into myths of whiteness and masculinity in the manner of an ephebe or warrior. In other words, the bad nigger type, though hypersexual as the macho, displays a retaliatory and accusatory race and gender ideal which is at odds with, indeed inassimilable to, the ideal of white masculinity because it renders whiteness unredeemable in the visibility of whiteness as contradiction and oppression. However, the bad nigger is wholly exploitable in the symbolic realm of escapist narrative and standardized forms of the Hollywood blaxploitation film. Therefore, the social and cultural contradiction of the unruly blackness and sexually and socially threatening black men of *Sweetback, Shaft, Superfly* and the likes are partially contained in cathartic celebration of them in the popular film form.

The bad nigger in the symbolic form of Blaxploitation indexes the rise of Black Power, the Black Arts Movement and an overall dissatisfaction with integration and the Civil Rights Movement (Bogle 1988 and 1973; Boyd 1997; Cripps 1993; Guerrero 1993; Reid 1993). Inherent in the Civil Rights *versus* the Black Arts debate is a class debate, a debate about the urban working class, the then defined underclass, and the social and cultural disenfranchisement of urban blacks, which in turn is a manifestation of an older Booker T. Washington *versus* W.E.B. DuBois debate about agrarian reform and the education of an intellectual class; furthermore, the

Civil Rights *versus* Black Arts Movement can be configured as a debate about masculine difference, as seen in the visual rhetoric of Sidney Poitier *versus* that of *Sweetback, Shaft,* or *Superfly.*

However, for the moment I would like to skirt this debate and highlight other aspects of Blaxploitation as a film form which inform the film history of Blaxploitation and inform my engagement with Blaxploitation and masculinity. In order to do this, I want to define briefly Blaxploitation and return to the questions of masculine difference through a discussion of Pam Grier and her rise in exploitation film

## BLAXPLOITATION: EXPLOITATION AND BLACKNESS

Thomas Doherty (1988) defines exploitation films as films which adhere to three discrete yet extended and coterminous elements of production and consumption: First, exploitation films are defined by their advertising and marketing, by their enticing promotions which capture audiences and lure them into the theatre; second, the exploitation film itself is both passive, as an object to be promoted and advertised, and active, as the subject engaging the target audience; and third, exploitation films are a kind of film which in turn implies that exploitation films have formal characteristics which differ from other films (3). The first element refers to exploitation proper. By this, Doherty means the advertising, press kits, marketing and publicity that accompany the release of any film. The second element is more specific to exploitation films which use exotic or sensitive subject matter, referring to the dialogic established between the film and its audience, or as Doherty notes: "The movie is said to 'exploit' an audience when it reflects onscreen the audience's expectation and values" (5).

The third element of the definition of the exploitation film is more complex and historically contingent upon Hollywood's production standards and aesthetic pretensions. In defining the contemporary notion of the exploitation film as a "kind" of film, "exploitation" refers to the strategy of both the formulaic (often remakes) and "timely and sensational" subject matter and the low budget production costs of an exploitation film (10).[6] As a kind of film, exploitation films are not content based or thematically structured in a manner in which one can argue that they visually or narratively organize a genre; however, exploitation films do formally communicate an aesthetic, organizing a cinematic expression across genres. Consequently, as Doherty argues, the three elements of "controversial content, bottom line bookkeeping, and demographic targeting—remain characteristic of any exploitation movie, whether scandalous material be aimed at 'adults' ('sexploitation'), Blacks ('blaxploitation'), or gorehounds ('axeploitation')" (10).

With this understanding of exploitation film as a production, marketing and aesthetic tradition, Blaxploitation is seen not only as the exploitation of the black audience and market, but also as the exploitation of the symbolic meanings of blackness, the symbolic meanings of race. With Poitier and the social problem film and Brown and the action film, blackness is exploited—given figurative and ethical meaning. However, Blaxploitation is an exegesis of blackness as a social symbol of controversy, scandal, sensation, escapism, and sex. In order to elaborate this point of the use of blackness in Blaxploitation, I digress, through an examination of Pam Grier. I take this digression through discussion of Grier because not only was she the most popular Blaxploitation star (amassing a greater number of films than any single male) but she was also one of the first stars wholly constructed as a draw for the black male audience. Therefore, an understanding of Grier's filmic construction, the use of race, the body and femininity in that construction, and ensuing debate around that construction provides insight into black filmic masculinity and the super bad nigger of Blaxploitation.

## THE QUEEN OF BLAXPLOITATION

Pam Grier started in sexploitation films. Sexploitation (as opposed to teen-pics and exploitation science fiction and horror) emerged in the late sixties and early seventies with the rise of drive-ins. As exploitation films, the early transgeneric cinematic expression of sexploitation films included ample nudity, but also a fair amount of sado-masochism, ersatz sexual intercourse (hetero-, bi- and homo-), and a considerable number of woman to woman brawls. As "drive-in flicks," their audience was young adult, mostly male. However, in keeping with the "timely" sensationalism of form, sexploitation films also deployed contemporary politics as part of their attraction. Hence, as Pam Cook (1993) notes, sexploitation films and exploitation films broadly, "celebrated in sexual role reversals in which strong assertive women, . . . , took their destiny in their own hands, . . . [and] dealt with social problems . . ." (xvi).

From this miasma of sex, violence, politics, and drive-in audiences, Pam Grier first rose to fame as prisoner/prison matron in a series of women's prison films. Women's prison films were generically defined by their location—a women's prison—and a varying narrative of escape and survival or imprisonment, survival and escape. Bordering on the pornographic, sexploitation films require of the actresses that their bodies, aside from bodily and facial gesture, perform through the use of race and body type. For the most part, the actress are all statuesque and white, with their weight, upper body and vocal register signifying various degrees of aggression or submission, class and education.

In Grier's early films, the women's prison is set in a far away, foreign jungle (mostly shot in the Philippines). Of the series in which Grier appears, she is the only black female and the only non-white character (except for male characters) with a speaking part. The exotic locales and the themes of female victimization, torture, and wrongful imprisonment construct a particular performance within the implicit *mise-en scène* of whiteness in which Grier, for lack of an other, becomes the exoticized other in a hierarchy of female (American female) imagery and bodily impersonation. As a consequence, Grier is called upon not only to be a gendered performative body, but also *the* performative racial body. As such, the black body, attached to the pre-significations of primitivism and hypersexuality, precipitate and participate in a hierarchy in which the black body, through its signification, performs the modalities of sexual practice (Muñoz 1995, 95). In other words, the racial body codes a preference, a tendency or sexual proclivity (as opposed to a person), which situated in a racial hierarchy, privileges the white female and male body as the site of the normative body, the normative object of desire. It is no surprise, therefore, to find that Grier's characters are all lesbians and/or sadomasochists. Through the racialization of sexual practice, the performance of race is congruent with the performance of sexual difference: To perform blackness is to perform sexuality, at the same time that the performance of whiteness and heterosexuality is erased *as performance.*

Blaxploitation, very simply as exploitative films do, offers no more than a reversal of racial hierarchy in order to capturing a target audience, priviledging the black body as the normative object of desire. But this priviledging of the black body undergoes shifts in *mise-en-scène* and narrative. The women's prison in a far away jungle becomes the black urban ghetto; the narrative of escape becomes the narrative of revenge and vendetta. A small change, indeed; however, it is important because the narrative of revenge and the black urban ghetto allows for the popular tenet of self-determination in the then current discourse of black power to be exploited in the narrative of retaliatory violence, at the same time that black power, and blackness, is signified as criminality and marginality.

During Grier's reign in sexploitation and the Blaxploitation Era, there was tremendous debate in the black public sphere about the purpose and value of these expressions of filmic blackness. In November 1975, Pam Grier, along with Tamara Dobson, Gloria Hendry, and Vonetta McGee, appeared on the cover of *Ebony*, in the title article "Battle among the Beauties" (Horton 1975). The article, which as the title indicates, highlights youth and beauty and frames Grier and her contemporaries within the then current debate about Blaxploitation and the presence of black actresses in Hollywood. These four actresses also framed as the "best and the brightest," owing to their consistent work and competitive professionalism. Of these four rising stars, Grier is presented as the most successful (at the time she was appearing simultaneously onscreen in *Black Mama, White Mama; Scream, Blacula, Scream;* and *Coffy*) with her five year contract at American International Pictures (AIP) (Horton, 146). The article provides a celebratory image of the four actresses, and particularly, Grier's image is constructed as one of a successful, sexy, energetic, and community oriented black actress.

The celebratory portrait of Grier is typical of *Ebony*'s seventies stance on black stars, and black public figures in general, and more indicative of the magazine's class stance, as opposed to its critical stance.[7] However, as the letters to the editor (*Ebony,* January 1974) indicate, Grier's image, as well as the images of Dobson, Hendry, and McGee, was far more complex and problematic (I will quote from only three of the letters):

1.  I have seen all four actresses . . . in their respective movies and I have yet to see any *real* acting from either of them. . . . I would rather have seen an article done on Cicely Tyson, a very serious, very black young actress (original emphasis).

2.  Even though I don't back your selection of actresses, you're definitely heading in the right direction. Let's have articles on Freda Payne, Rosalind Cash or Brenda Skyes [other actresses working at the time]. . . .

3.  It's understandable that black actors and actresses get involved in some mean competition with each other and fire heavy ammunition, but I don't think there's a need to extend the throatcutting process to readers trying to get a halfway decent concept of black actresses in Hollywood . . . (*Ebony,* January 1974, 8).

These letters situate the actresses in a larger intertext of talent, class, and community and public responsibility. Even though this dialog is internal and between *Ebony* and its black community of readers, it reflects the broader sense of double consciousness which the "black" in black star signifies.

The notion of double consciousness as it mediates and is articulated in the *Ebony* article and in the letters to the editors situate the images of Blaxploitation within a history of star images and community of stars in which, on the one hand, "talent" is emblematic of blackness and consciousness of double consciousness (Cicely Tyson as a "very serious, very black young actress") and in which, on the other hand, success is owing to and in exchange with the community of black stars (the letter requesting more attention to the younger rising black actresses and requesting less reportage of the "throatcutting" process required in achieving fame).

However, the article, "Battle among the Beauties," is also an extension of a preceding article in *Ebony*'s then ongoing debate about the ethical and aesthetic value of Blaxploitation films. In "New Films: Culture or Con Game," J.B. Mason (*Ebony*, December 1972) debates the use-value of Blaxploitation's representations of black men and women. Mason ultimately asks who produces the pictures, who economically benefits, and how many black people, outside of a few directors and actors and actresses, are employed in Hollywood—questions of economics and self-determination. Through the use of interviews with actors, actresses and directors, Mason poses and counter-poses two communities of black stars, the older more established, more critically acclaimed stars (for example the article quotes Beah Richards, Cicely Tyson, Ossie Davis and Poitier) alongside and against the Blaxploitation stars (Fred Williamson, Jim Brown, and Ron O'Neal). Again the tropes of talent and quality are evoked as a public instanciation and display of a responsible blackness and cast against the tropes of the "superbad ass nigger" and "super mama" stereotypes of blackness embodies in the characters of Blaxploitation.

The letters to the editor (*Ebony*, February and March 1973) in response to Mason's article both echo and refute the article's sentiment, but the letters also suggest that the debate about images is futile in and of itself (I will only quote four letters):

1. I was especially moved by your article, 'The new films: culture or con game?,' . . . as I have been seething with wrath and staring in disbelief ever since the emergence of *Sweetback* and the succeeding trash to which it gave rise. . . . [I]s it not yet evident to Gordon Parks Jr. and Sr., Melvin Van Peebles *et. al.*, that the fruit of their labor (no matter how well conceived, symbolically projected or profitable) is literally MURDERING a generation of black youths? (original emphasis) (*Ebony*, March 1973, 18).

2. All the black organization leaders who are against a black movie such as *Super Fly* obviously moved from the ghetto and forgot 'what's goin on.' To be ashamed and embarrassed by the truth is to be brain-washed (*ibid.*).

3.  I'm totally disgusted with the voices that have risen up in Black
    America denouncing *Super Fly* and making *Sounder* seem angelic.
    It seems that middle class and misled blacks can't deal with a
    black man such as Priest. . . . [Middle class and misled blacks] feel
    uneasy because they feel it reflects on them . . . [b]ut black people
    that live in ghettos can relate to that because it's not as fantasized
    as it seems . . . (*ibid.*, February 1973, 16).

4.  It seems that the NAACP, CORE, and PUSH are convinced that
    the movie industry is a major concern of black people. I am of the
    opinion that open housing, equal education, equal employment,
    law with justice, fair representation and economic growth, for the
    attainment of which these organizations were founded, are still
    the main unresolved issues of today's blacks . . . (*ibid.*, March
    1973, 17).

The debate is either a much-needed moral charge against blacks working in
Hollywood, a self-serving, opposing response to films about "real" black
folks, or little more than a diversion from the pressing demands of the
immediate civil and political disenfranchisement of black people in the
nation at large.

The resulting figures of the black star that emerge in the field of view
of *Ebony* and its readers are the simultaneous articulation of the need for
control of filmic image production and the contradictory articulation of a
two-tier, class inflected black star system. This two-tier system is in keeping
with Hollywood's production standards of A and B movies stars (and as a
success story, the rise to stardom is always a class ascent); however, form
behind the veil of racial consciousness and the cultural politics of self-determination and "race responsibility," the two-tier system emerges with the A
star as the middle class "noble savage" image of choice and the second rate
B star as the more authentic "pusher from the ghetto" that is more "real"
representation of the black experience and lived-world.

I have gone through this discussion of Pam Grier in order to elaborate
the object of blackness which is appropriated in Blaxploitation, to elaborate
the questions that Blaxploitation raised for the black filmgoers and in the
black public sphere, and to broaden the field in which the masculine figures
of Blaxploitation were situated. Films like *Sweetback*, *Shaft*, and *Superfly*
(and even *Cotton Comes to Harlem* and *Across 110ᵗʰ Street*) served as pre-
cursory forms of Blaxploitation, providing an aesthetic, a documentary style,
a *mise-en-scène* of blackness and a content base which was exploited for
profit. The blackness of these independent and studio productions' industrial

progeny (productions like *Blacula, Coffy, Black Cesar,* etc.) undergoes a shift in the figurative plane, a shift from the representation of black people to the representation of people as black. Blackness becomes a cinematic ethos or an aura, an expression of an Adornoian "jargon of authenticity," emptied of its expressivity of existence and existential crisis, rendering reified images as expressions of empowerment.

As a consequence, the black men and women of Blaxploitation, the Super Bad Nigger and Super Bad Mama, become figures of the inauthentic, at the same time that they are an expression of authenticity. The male characters become narrative archetypes, substituting black men in the position of hero and anti-hero. The subsequent morality of the narrative outcome, the morality of autonomy, self-determination, and community, is seemingly natural and just, however escapist and self-exploiting. As Adorno notes of this inauthentic authenticity in *The Jargon of Authenticity:* "Mediated and immediate elements [like Blaxploitation, blackness and the current of Black Power and the Black Arts Movement] are mediated through each other in frightful ways. And since they are synthetically prepared, that which is mediated has become the caricature of what is natural" (Adorno 1973, 19). In this light Blaxploitation performs a kind of dubbing of blackness onto generic narratives and conventions, translating them into a cinematic blackness.

However, it is in the dubbing of blackness and the contradictory inauthentic gestures of authenticity which foreground the ethical valuations of gender and race in Blaxploitation. Race is given a moral valence in the differentiation and relegations of masculinities. Degrees and graduations of masculinity, however ostensible or false, re-deploy discourses of the noble savage, the civilized *versus* the primitive and the divided whole, establishing the trope of reconciliation and integration into a whole or ideal gender as a figurative goal. It is through reconciliation and the signifying of race as an ethical problematic that black masculinity is elevated into the overall range of masculine difference. Yet, as Blaxploitation is an exaltation of symbolic blackness, the ethical dimensions of race and gender posited in the array of masculine difference and the insertion of black men into that array is rendered counterproductive in that Blaxploitation serves to re-articulate, renew and reaffirm stereotypical, hyperreal imagery in the expediency of escapist narratives.

# Chapter Four

# Boyz, Boyz, Boyz: New Black Cinema and Black Masculinity

The notion of New Black Cinema is a periodization, drawing on and expanding Tommy Lott's (1991) demarcation of Black Cinema: Early Films (1890–1920); Early Soundies and Race Film (1920–1945); Post-War Problem Films (1945–1965); The L.A. Rebellion (roughly 1967–1975); and Contemporary Films, which I refer to as New Black Cinema (roughly 1985 to present). New Black Cinema as a period of black film roughly begins with Spike Lee's *She's Gotta Have It* (1986) and is further marked by the participation of a second generation (second to the LA Rebellion filmmakers) of film school trained filmmakers like Lee, Reginald and Warrington Hudlin, John Singleton, and Robert Townsend. However, the question remains: what is new about New Black Cinema? The "new" in New Black Cinema refers to the moment of emergence and the productive and aesthetic outcome of this moment. Useful in understanding this moment are three convergent ideas: Trey Ellis's (1989a) manifesto on the "New Black Aesthetic"; Cornel West's (1990) "new cultural politics of difference"; and Manthia Diawara's (1993a) formal analysis of black film's "new realism."

In 1989, Trey Ellis's (1989a and b) "The New Black Aesthetic" identified a current of cultural production which included not only film, but also music, literature and theatre.[1] For Ellis the New Black Aesthetic, also known as the NBA, was a revival in the black arts, a "[synthesis of] the last two black art revivals, the Harlem Renaissance and the Black Arts Movement" (Ellis 1989b, 250). Black artists educated in a post-Civil Rights era, artists who were characterized as "cultural mulattoes," black artists who were either raised or educated in middle class, predominately

white communities, fueled the NBA. These cultural mulattoes were the
first generation middle class products of integration:

> Just as a genetic mulatto is a black person of mixed parents who can
> often get along fine with his white grandparents, a cultural mulatto,
> educated by a multi-racial mix of cultures, can also navigate easily in
> the white world.

Furthermore, this class of black artist is, because of its class status, a transcendent critical device:

> For the first time in our history we are producing a critical mass of col-
> lege graduates who are children of college graduates themselves. Like
> most artistic booms, the NBA is a post-bourgeois movement driven by
> second generation of middle class. Having scraped their way to relative
> wealth and, too often, crass materialism, our parents have freed (or
> compelled) us to bite those hands that fed us and sent us to college
> (1989a, 239).

The prophets of the NBA were aggressively culturally antagonistic, celebrating a complicated and confrontational blackness. And as Tera Hunter
(1989) noted in response to Ellis's NBA, the abbreviation, NBA, indicates
that it is, at least as outlined in the manifesto, an overwhelmingly masculine
art movement, and therefore, already inherently problematic in its construction and history (247–249).

As if to answer both Ellis and Hunter, the new cultural politics of difference provides a historical framework for elaborating movements like the
New Black Aesthetic. For Cornell West (1990), the new cultural politics of
difference is a creative, artistic, and intellectual response to a global
moment of the decline of the West and the re-territorialization of the late
capitalist, post-colonial, post communist cultural terrain. The new cultural
politics of difference is contingent, historical and strategic. Or as West
notes:

> The new cultural politics of difference is neither simply oppositional in
> contesting the mainstream . . . for inclusion, nor transgressive in the
> avant-gardist sense of shocking conventional bourgeois audience. It
> embraces the distinct articulations of talented (and usually privileged)
> contributors to culture who desire to align themselves with demoral-
> ized, demobilized, depoliticized and disorganized people in order to
> empower and enable social action and, if possible, to enlist collective

insurgency for the expansion of freedom, democracy and individuality. This perspective impels these cultural critics and artists to reveal, as an integral component of their production, the very operations of power within their immediate work contexts (academy, museum, gallery, mass media). Thus while linking their activities to the fundamental, structural overhaul of these institutions, they often remain financially dependent on them. . . . For these critics of culture, theirs is a gesture that is simultaneously progressive and co-opted (19–20).

West continues further to identify intellectual, existential and political challenges and provocations facing cultural practitioners in this phase of new cultural politics. The intellectual challenge is one in which cultural practitioners are asked to question the modes of representation in terms of their production. For African Americans and African diasporians the first response was a "mode of resistance that was *moralistic in content* and *communal in character* [original italics]," an engagement with positive imagery, stereotypes and misrepresentations, and accordingly: "These images 're-presented' monolithic and homogeneous Black communities, in a way that could displace past misrepresentations of these communities" (27). Though this moralistic response was a first, West, by tracing this response through various contemporary permutations, elaborates the appropriate response to the intellectual challenge as one of "prophetic criticism": " . . . [prophetic criticism] begins with social structural analyses it also makes explicit its moral and political aims. It is partisan, partial, engaged and crisis-centered, yet always keeps open a skeptical eye to avoid dogmatic traps, premature closures, formulaic formulation or rigid conclusions" (31).

The existential challenge is one of acquisition and survival: How to acquire the skills, tools and finances to produce. For this challenge, West identifies the new cultural politics of difference practitioner as a critical organic catalyst (33). This person is a moral, political and intellectual exemplar well versed in the popular and elite forms and grounded in enabling forms of criticism and artistic praxis. Finally, the political challenge is one of coalition formation and avoiding the "immoral patriarchal, imperial, jingoistic and xenophobic constraints" of dominant cultural identities (35). In short, the new politics of cultural difference produces the artist, intellectual, and cultural critic as a kind of modernist *flâneur* in the suit of the post-modernist "New World *bricoleurs*" (36).

The third contextual "new" providing the discursive foundation for discussion of New Black Cinema is Manthia Diawara's new realism. Through a reading of American film history and the formal strategies of black independent film, Diawara proposes "two paradigms of black cinema aesthetics," two aesthetic trajectories in which the conventional and Hollywood classical narrative dimensions of time and space are deployed and re-deployed as black cinematic statements. For Diawara, space and time become vectors of re-schematization and re-thematization:

> Black films use spatial narration as a way of revealing and linking
> Black spaces that have been separated and suppressed by White times,
> and as a means of validating Black culture. . . .
>     The emphasis on time, on the other hand, reveals the Black American
> as he/she engenders him/herself amid the material condition of everyday life in American society (13).

Diawara continues further to categorize the spatially re-oriented, at times non-linear, narratives (e.g., *Daughters of the Dust*) as "expressive and celebratory of Black culture," and the temporally re-orientated, linear ("Blacktimes narrative") narratives as "existentialist performances of Black people against policing, racism, and genocide" (13).

It is Diawara's second category of "time-based" narratives that are of interest for discussion here. For these narratives are inevitably masculinist narratives of coming of age and rites of passage. Indeed, Diawara emphasizes the black narrative of *rites de passage* specifically in reference to *Boyz N the Hood*. It is in this discussion that Diawara elaborates the New Black Realism: "In these films [*Juice, Deep Cover, Boyz N the Hood*], . . . to be a man is to be responsible for the Black community, and to protect it against the aforementioned dangers [genocide, drugs, the police, criminality]" (24). And furthermore:

> The new realism films imitate the existent reality of urban life in America. Just as in real life the youth are pulled between hip hop life style,
> gang life, and education, we see in the films neighborhoods that pulled
> between gang members, rappers, and education-prone kids. For the
> black youth, the passage into manhood is also a dangerous enterprise
> which leads to death both in reality and in film (25).

The three critical frameworks, the New Black Aesthetic, new cultural politics of difference, and New Black Realism, provide the overlapping, interconnected and discursive grid for discussion of the period identified as New Black Cinema. Furthermore, this grid is used to examine New Black Cinema and the cultural production of filmic black masculinity.[2] An understanding of the cultural and nationalistic legacies of the New Black Aesthetic; the contemporary cultural formations and histories of the new cultural politics of difference; and the aesthetic strategies and their continuities and discontinuities within cinema and narrative as outlined in New Black Realism allows for a deeper, more specific description of the construction of race and masculinity at work in New Black Cinema. Also, by understanding these three vectors of the "new," film and cinema are revealed as a practice engaged in a dialectical real/representation relation, a dialectic between the symbolic and the social in which representation is active and interactive—not just entertaining and reflective—, and at the same time instructive and constructive of social meaning.

This brings me to my project and a critical look at New Black Cinema. In the Hollywood tradition of "mainstream film," the visual codes surrounding blacks and blackness on the screen have been stereotypical images, more contemporarily drug dealers, prostitutes, single mothers and complacent drag queens. These are the traditional encodings informed by popular discourse of race and gender, reflecting and sustaining popular convictions about blackness and black sexuality. In the realm of popular culture, these discursive images, as film transcodes them, dispense the "framework[s] of symbols, concepts and images through which we understand, interpret, and represent aspects of our 'racial' existence" (Omi 1989 114). However, since the mid-1980s, Hollywood and independent American cinema have seen a rise in films by African American filmmakers. Often touted as being "by, for, and about African Americans," these films are social commentaries, indictments of racism and depictions of "everyday" African American lives. Afrocentrism and nationalistic pride often inform the aesthetic frameworks of these films, and they are replete with black cultural signifiers.

Juxtaposed against the traditional representations of blacks and blackness, New Black Cinema takes on the project of cultural intervention and the recoding of blackness, "revising the visual codes surrounding black skin on the screen and in the public realm" (Snead, Program 23, 1–2). This is ultimately a political project within its relationship to the Hollywood tradition and the traditional racialist and, at times, racist codings of blackness and one which is dialectical within the real/representation relationship of New Black Cinema. My interest is in the representational dialogic of racial difference within film and the real/representation dialectic of cultural, gender and sexual identity.

The number of films that I have viewed in preparation for discussion raises various complicated issues of race, class and gender and the representation of race, class and gender, ranging from sexual liberation in Spike Lee's successful independent film, *She's Gotta Have It,* to the coming of age story in John Singleton's *Boyz N the Hood*.[3] At the core of these films' complexities are the problematics and paradoxes of black masculinity and images of black men and black masculinity. The operation of recoding masculinity from established, now historic, Hollywood codings of black men and black masculinity visualizes a more ambiguous, more discursive image, producing the meanings of an intricately constructed masculinity, more complexly dimensional than the submissive, docile Tom or the morally corrupt, conniving, sexually threatening drug dealer.[4]

However, these more aggressive, politically charged black masculinities, now turned difficult, involved, ideological metaphors, construct themselves, in the arena of meanings, from the existing, pop cultural and filmic representations of masculinity. By operating referentially to the popular cultural images of black men which are visibly recurring, or simply fixed, instructing homogeneous, monolithic, and culturally familiar (and therefore, quite culturally consumable) constructs, the critical attention that New Black Cinema markets as black men and masculinity then seemingly becomes reenforcement of singular, monologic meanings, only within different popular images. What is culturally familiar—hip-hop, rap music, commodified neo-nationalism and the cool posed, "endangered black man"—becomes representationally and culturally totalized as the Black Experience of the young, heterosexual urban black man, the only experience possible.

I have chosen to examine three of the earliest New Black Cinema films: Spike Lee's musical, *School Daze;* Reginald and Warrington Hudlin's teenpic, *House Party;* and John Singleton's coming of age tale, *Boyz N the Hood*. I have chosen these three films for the purposes of critiquing the discursive visual recodings of black masculinity. I have selected these three particular films because the codings and recodings of masculinity and black masculinity are different across the genres of musical, teen comedy and the more literary coming of age story. By examining these three films in a sequential order, I propose to interrogate patterns of formation of black masculinity as these patterns position (and re-position) women and female sexuality, male homosexuality and the patriarchal construction of the family. These films, if unmediated, serve to construct a master narrative of black men and masculinity and sexuality that attempts to be seamless, unitary and phallic.

## SCHOOL DAZE

"This film is . . . about our existence as a people in white America"[5]

*School Daze* is a musical, but not quite what one might expect. As Toni Cade Bambara (1991) notes: "Lee . . . chooses an enshrined genre of the dominant cinema . . . whose conventions were not designed to address an embattled community's concerns" (49). In the big MGM Hollywood tradition of elaborate sets, choreography, pageantry and spectacle, *School Daze* is a musical fused with the black cultural signifiers of jazz, Motown sound, and D.C. go-go. Using an all black, ensemble cast, the musical takes place during the homecoming events on the fictional campus of the historically black Mission College.

The focus of the film revolves around four gendered social groups: The Gammites, men; the Wannabees, women; Dap and da fellas, men; and the Jigaboos, women. The tension of the film lies in the shade/caste/class racial identity and community conflict that subdivides, and heterosexually aligns, the gendered groups into two binaries: the Jigaboos, the dark skinned group, led by Dap and Rachel, made up of predominately working class black folk *versus* the Wannabees, led by Julien and Jane, made up of light skinned, upwardly mobile, middle class black folk. The women confront the shade complex and racial identity issue. What is at stake is who, culturally, is the "blackest," has internalized white aesthetics of beauty more, and is more naturally black. The men confront the class and community division, as one of who is going to lead black people what political ideology will inform a people's cultural and economic mobility. The campus is divided along these lines, representing the political and cultural dilemma of black communities at large.

Thus in keeping with the popular, yet oppositional, cultural positionality of New Black Cinema, the musical takes place during the homecoming events on the Mission College campus, examining the politics of race in an embattled community. It is in this setting that Lee subverts the use of the musical. Richard Dyer (1981) analyzes entertainment, and particularly the Hollywood musical, as utopian fantasies inverting the signifiers of scarcity, exhaustion, dreariness, manipulation and fragmentation with the utopian sensibilities of abundance, energy, intensity, transparency, and community.[6] The entertaining inversions finally serve as temporal and spatial escapes from the "inadequacies of the society." With the musical, the result is a "utopian world" in which tension and conflict resolve in a burst into dance and song.

Dyer further notes that the "utopian world" of entertainment responds to real needs in society, but entertainment is also defining and delimiting what is a legitimate, real need in society. What is defined out of the category of "real need" within the utopian vision of entertainment are the social-cultural problems of race and gender, among other things. Spike Lee disrupts the musical form by placing the problem of race and racial identity into the field of vision, and by orienting this disruption in the utopian sensibility of community, the problem of race and racial disunity is then seen as an imped-iment and hindrance to community formation and function within an oppressive environment. Though Lee disrupts the utopianism inherent in the musical form, *School Daze* is not simply an alternate dystopian vision of the world in that it does not represent the imaginary as a wretched, fearful place. The disruption of the form allows for the representation of a black commu-nity as a thinking, self-critical body of people.

However, as the film is not a dystopian one, it is a masculinist one. The political question and possibility of unification seems to be the debate of the film, and by positioning the unification of black people and black communi-ties within a narrative history of slavery, emancipation, reconstruction, migrations, segregation, civil rights and economic plight (all of which are set in the photo montage as the film's credits appear on screen), *School Daze* and the question of unification then flow into a cultural current of self-determina-tion and survival. With the Afrocentric vision, nationalist iconography, and urban, hip-hop cultural infusions, the fluent visual, rhythms and language of the film become messengers for the unification of a retrograde nation, a nation informed by the patriarchal demarcations of power and gender inher-ent in the nationalistic agenda (Mosse 1985). As informed by the ideological and sexual paradigms of cultural nationalism, sexual difference becomes the discourse mediating intraracial relations, separating racial identity and com-munity into heterosexual, gendered domains. Racial identity, the light/dark conflict is feminine and signified by the female body; community and leader-ship are masculine. Unification then falls into the traditional construction of racial oppression and the recovery from racial oppression as a "man's prob-lem," as racial emasculation, as the recovery of the phallus. It is in this visual construction of race, racial identity and community that I want to discuss the representation of the female body.

The women's color/shade problem is introduced in the first musical number, "Straight and Nappy." In the narrative, the two groups of women, the Jigaboos, the dark skinned women and the Wannabees, the light skinned women, confront each other in the dormitory corridor. What ensues through the musical number is an argument over shade, weaves, naps, contact lens and men. In "Madame Ree Ree's Hair Salon," the Jigaboos and Wannabees are in a gang fight set to the sound of big band. The territory of dispute is the female body, the black female body. Rachel, Dap's girlfriend and head Jigaboo, and Jane, Julian's girlfriend and head Wannabee, face off to the chorus: "Talkin' 'bout good and bad hair/whether you are dark or fair/go on and swear/see if I care/good and bad hair."

At one point in the number, the Jigaboos and the Wannabees don fans bearing images of Hattie McDaniel/Mammy and Vivian Leigh/Scarlet O'Hara, the perennial Hollywood images of the black woman *versus* the white woman. The fans of McDaniel and Leigh as they circulate within the spectacle serve as the choice for the women, neither one of which is a real choice for black women. The racialized masquerade, as indicated by the donning of fans, directs the spectator to the constructedness of women and racialized femininity and to the female body as the demarcation of the color difference and intraracial community problem. The female body is spectacle, objectified, scandalous, and contemptible. The spectacle of "Straight and Nappy" is cathartic in that it removes the skin color conflict of racial identity from the men and embodies it in the female body. Racial identity is then separated from the community of men, becoming an object for recovery.

Not surprisingly, in the narrative of the film, Rachel and Dap argue in the course of which Rachel suggests that Dap only dates her because of the shade, the darkness, of her skin. Rachel argues that Dap's association with her, "the darkest thing on campus," is "good for [his] all-the-way-down pro-black image." The female body and the skin color/shade of the female body become commodities in exchange for power and control. As commodities, certain values are assigned. In this case there is the historic value of white over black, light over dark. The skin color/shade of the objectified woman, now the black body, determines the politic of the man in possession of the body.

A more explicit example than the demonstrated use of Rachel's body is the use of Jane's body in the Gammites rights of passage. After the pledges go over, joining the fraternity and becoming Gamma men, Half-Pint (Spike Lee's character) is still a virgin. What follows is Julian's (the head Gamma) trickery and coercion of both Jane and Half-Pint: Jane is raped/her body exchanged for Half-Pint's virginity with what she bodily posses: His manhood and his racial identity. Half-Pint, now a Gamma man, enters into the ranks of the future leaders of the race. The sexual act, his initiation into manhood, recuperates his authenticity, his blackness, and his political alignment with the Wannabees, as a class and as a community.

Even though Lee's disruption of the musical form allows for an interrogation and re-presentation of the representation of black masculinity, Lee does not subvert the male gaze (however, he does racialize it).[7] Operating in a classic narrative form, the images of the women remain static, eroticized and fragmented; the men are active agents, representing movement and resolution. Race and sexual difference are collapsed; the black woman then simultaneously represents the lack of blackness and the phallus. Consequently, race and sexual difference are fetishized. Sexual difference becomes containment in a conventional construction of masculinity.

## HOUSE PARTY

> I wanted to make a movie that had social messages, but was also entertaining, nonstop fun. . . . [8]

In Warrington and Reginald Hudlin's *House Party*, coding of male homosexuality and the representation of the male homosexual both situate the recoding of black masculinity as racial and class responsibility. *House Party* is a teenpic as characterized by the simple plot, the narrative of the rebellious youth, submerged in the urban, counter-cultural lifestyle of the day, the rhythms of hip-hop and rap. This is a very deliberate film, very much in dialogue with Hollywood, mainstream film and popular cultural images of black people, especially black men, and very conscious of its youthful black audience. Therefore, what is very formulaic and exploitative (of teenagers, music and adolescent angst) in a Hollywood convention is rendered critical and interventionist, foregrounding race and oppression.

What is so deliberate and intentional about this film is the inversion of the common, stereotypical representations of black men and black communities with opposing cultural codings that, in turn, bring into question the fabrication and falsity of the stereotype itself. These critical inversion leads Lisa Kennedy (1990) to comment: "[*House Party*] touches on many of the signs of the black familiar—the projects, police brutality, teen sex, teen drinking, . . . black on black crime,. . . ." By "touching" on these signs of the "black familiar," and inverting them, the Hudlins construct a cinematic portrait of a utopian, "imagined community," inventing the visual meaning of a nation of black people, in which the stereotypes are supplanted, in the case of this film, with revised, "positive" images: There is the single parent family with a black man, Pop, who is the head of the household in contrast to the much, media dogged single black mother; there is the absence of a drug-plagued, inner city black ghetto, replaced by the sanitary, drug free suburban community; class strife is submerged; the black middle class is attendant and responsible for the entire representational community; and there is the representation of sexually responsible black youth.

Kid, the protagonist, is introduced to the audience as the only child in a male-headed household, trustworthy, and obedient, a clean-cut young man. This introduction is determining of two things: First, it establishes the narrative of the teen film as one of disobedience; the acting out of disobedience and punishment becomes the narrative motivation and plot closure for the film. Second, the family setting with Pop, as the widower father, is in opposition to the abandoned, single black mother image that is so pervasive in the media and Hollywood representation of the black family (which leaves the image of the single black mother intact and unexamined, simply suggesting that a man is better). Placing Kid next to Pop and suspending them in idiomatic language and the hip-hop culture codings of the *mise-en-scène*, Kid and Pop become authentic community role models for black youth. The role model itself offers a unitary symbol of man, black man, and manhood, informing class, sexual, and aesthetic standards to which the nation is to aspire and maintain. Respectability, as in Kid's responsibility in sexual abstinence and respect to and for his father, defines the parameters of moral codes, what is acceptable, not acceptable, what is good or bad. The role model, then, becomes a form of social control delimiting the parameters and the permanence of the construct of the black man.

As a role model, Kid's disobedience must be a punishable and redeemable learning experience. In the cafeteria scene immediately following his introduction, Kid wrangles with thugs—Stab, Zilla, and Pee Wee. The premise: Kid accidentally spills milk, a sexual slur is directed at this mother, and finally the pheromonal battle cry, issued simultaneously from Stab, Zilla and Pee Wee: "I smell pussy!" Thus, Kid is effeminized. The "smell of pussy" leads to a fight, in which Kid is beaten and reprimanded and Stab is expelled. As the film continues, it becomes clear that the premise of the film, Kid's going to the party without his father's consent, is ultimately a test of his manhood.

Now I want to turn the discussion to a close reading of two of the film's discursive maneuvers: the manipulation of the presence of homosexuality and the absence of the homosexual in this film. Homosexuality is present and detached from the black man and the black community. This presence and detachment serves two purposes. First, there is the establishment of homosexuality as a deviation from and threat to heterosexual black masculinity. When Kid is arrested, the responsible heterosexual sex scene in which the use of the condom, the trope of safe sex, is solely contraceptive precedes the jail scene, which is ostensibly about safe sex and anti-rape. The fixed use of the condom as contraception without a hint of its prophylactic use reconfigures any configured safe sex message, as it re-inscribes heterosexuality. What is articulated in the homosocial jailhouse setting of leering, caged men is that homosexuality is solely a homosexual act of violence and rape—with AIDS as the signifier of a wrongful act of violence. (Not surprisingly, the discourse of AIDS is conducted in the confines of a jail cell as something arrested and criminal in the black community.[9])

The second use of homosexuality lies in the submerged text of class difference. If homosexuality is a metaphor for the conflict between black men and criminality, the metaphor of disavowal, then metaphor intersects with metonym at the point of class. Class is submerged in a discourse of heterosexual, masculine difference and is defined, and subsequently undefined, by the removal of homosexuality and the differentiation of a good, straight black man from a bad, straight black man, a positive image from a negative image. The presence of homosexuality demonstrates a black masculinity that is fluid between the heterosexual poles of good and bad. The concealment of class difference behind the veil of a good/bad dualism and pervasive morality refigures class on a moral plane transcoding the accoutrement and the materiality of class into moral signs. In this refiguration "Jheri" curls, bulging muscles, tank tops, and dark skin, the working class signifiers of black masculinity, become the signifiers of the morally corrupt. The narrative identification of Kid as the protagonist positions spectators to identify with middle class righteousness, priviledging the middle class aesthetic of the film.

Curiously missing in the presence of homosexuality is its embodiment in the homosexual. The absence of the homosexual, the lack of the physical display or some textual disclosure of a character, is deceptive in that the physical absence itself gives presence to the homosexual. I mean that homosexuals, specifically gay men, are not in the film, but figuratively still there. The first three gay men appear on the body of Bilial, the dj for the evening's infamous party. Bilial is bedecked with Keith Haring "Free South Africa" buttons, the oversized Willi Smith clothing, and Patrick Kelly designer buttons and combs.[10] These three men, a pop artist and two designers, respectively, were all dying or had already died of AIDS by the release of *House Party.* All three of these men were gay; two of them, Willi Smith and Patrick Kelly, were black. During the jail scene, the last two gay men, Rock Hudson and Liberace, appear in reference to their deaths from AIDS.

The presence of the absent homosexual totalizes the coding of black men and masculinity as unitary and heterosexual. Gay black men, for example Willi Smith and Patrick Kelly, are commodified and erased, in the appropriated commodity form, from the representational black community, and gay white men, Rock Hudson and Liberace, signify the homosexual body. The cathexis of the homosexuality onto the absent, white, male homosexual body negates the possibility of a black gay man. Of course in view of the jail cell finale, the absent homosexual body, indeed the performative body, is doubly negated from the black community as it is contained within the film's insidious AIDS discourse, a discourse of criminality, confinement and race.

Again, as with *School Daze,* there is an oppositional aesthetic which foregrounds race and the construction of race, only to re-inscribe race in a discourse of patriarchy and heterosexuality. The reversal of denigrating stereotypes into the positive role model character of Kid is problematic in that the role model and role model-ing is generative of another stereotype, perhaps more moral and corrective, but nonetheless a stereotype—a fixed and fixing conventional conception of black masculinity. The positive/negative image abstraction, as conceived, only serves to transpose one stereotype with another. The positive stereotype of black is exchanged with the negative stereotype of white. This limits the film's visual analysis of social messages to an us/them binary opposition, replacing "them" (white folk) with "us" (black folk), without interrogating the construct of us/them. The blind sighted contradiction of this binary opposition is the re-inscription of the oppressor and the oppressed, or as in the film, heterosexual, masculine subject formation as determined by the negation of the homosexual.

## BOYZ N THE HOOD

My film has a lot of messages in it . . . but my main message is that African American men have to take responsibility for raising their children, especially their boys. Fathers have to teach their boys to be men. The audience will be able to see the direction that the characters take when there is an absence or a presence of fathers in their lives.[11]

In *Boyz N the Hood,* John Singleton employs some of the narrative conventions of the melodrama, as Jackie Bayars (1991) has outlined them, which provide a mode for constructing moral identity. As Bayars explains, the melodramatic form functions as a site of conflict over social values, is often situated in family struggle, and often serves to define and redefine gender and its relationship to the structure of the family (8). Bayars also discusses the male-oriented melodramas in which men are coming of age and establishing identity and relationships with their fathers (217–226). In a traditional reading, a masculine coming of age story follows a young man as he finds himself, establishes his masculinity, and masters his sexual awakening and sexual urges (Rutherford 1988, 21–67). *Boyz N the Hood* does not break with this tradition; however, in an expansion of the notion of family to an inclusion of community, the film places the story in South Central Los Angeles, an urban black community. Again as with *School Daze* and *House Party* race is centered, central to the melodrama.

Unlike *School Daze* and *House Party, Boyz* does not use sexual difference and sexuality, women and homosexuality, to define and negotiate
black masculinity and black men. In turn, in the absence of homosexuality
and with the oppositional symbolism of father and mother, black men are
defined against heterosexual, masculine differences, and once defined black
men are presented in an Oedipal opposition to black women as mothers in
a family structure. This distinction of the definition by differences in masculinity is crucial because it then is the cause for the filmic opposition of
black man and women.

First I want to examine the men, Furious, Tre Ricky and Doughboy.
There is a parental figure, Furious, from whom the codings of masculinity
and the fraternal order of Tre, Ricky, and Doughboy is derivative. The representation of black men and masculinity is in dialog with the representation of male heterosexuality. In this dialogue the film gives an age and
maturation continuum of black men. This allows the audience to see the
men through childhood adolescence and manhood. This also allows for the
visualization of difference in black men, how this difference, supposedly,
develops and how finally, the singular image of black man is created.

The difference in masculinity pivots on the representation of Doughboy. As a visual image, Doughboy is both narratively and aesthetically
abject, the low point, the lost, the dispossessed, the visually banished, yet
not disavowed, forcing, but not bursting, the seams of masculinity: Doughboy is very much a black man, not removed from the film's range of black
masculinity, but nonetheless, not what a black man should be.

Within the narrative Doughboy is the bad seed, the disfavored son of
Ms. Baker; his is unemployed and criminal. Aesthetically, and in contrast to
the well built, toned and well groomed images of Tre and Ricky (Doughboy's brother), Doughboy differs in that he is fat and physically sloppy,
malt liquor totting and "Jheri" curled, all the trappings that have come to
code the masculinity of black underclass.

As the abject, Doughboy defines the possibility of black masculinity,
indeed the nadir, which is descendent from Furious, the peak of black masculinity. This construction of masculinity, with its highs and lows, allows
for the totalizing monolith of Furious as the father and re-claimer. For, once
abject-ed, Doughboy challenges and narratively motivates the re-construc-
tion of masculinity. Consequently, Furious must meet the challenge by raising his son, Tre, as only a man can, and since Furious is the only father,
absent or present in the film, as only he can.

To Singleton's credit, the audience is not bombarded with heavy, and
naively simplistic, good/bad moralism. Doughboy's abjection is not represented as bad in that he is not good, but Doughboy is an anti-hero, conscious

of his abjection, knowing of his environment and mastering of it. As the rejected son and the ex-con, doughboy creates his own community of men in which he is the leader and protector. On the fringes of black masculinity, beyond recovery, Doughboy defines black masculinity and, while avenging his brother's murder, redeems black masculinity.

At the core of the representation of masculine difference and the reconstruction and reclamation of black masculinity is the representation of women and the family and family values. The singular father image of Furious is projected against that of three images of the mother, Ms. Baker, the crack mother and Reva, Furious' ex-wife. While Furious is the instructive, politically aware, community based entrepreneur, Ms. Baker, Ricky and Doughboy's mother, is a single mother with no narrative means of income. Doughboy as the abject is the product of a female headed, single parent household. In contrast to Furious' parental guidance and Afrocentric encouragements of self-determination, Ms. Baker favors Ricky over Doughboy, giving some guidance and encouragement to Ricky and nothing but verbal abuse to Doughboy. The only other neighborhood mother that we see is the crack mother across the street. This is the mother who allows her young child to wander, unattended, into traffic. This is the mother who offers fellatio to buy crack.

Reva, Tre's mother, who gives her son up to Furious because she feels she is unable to raise her man child, later in the film, surrounded by the professional, single woman opulence of her plush apartment, is depicted as upwardly mobile and meddling, opportunistic in her request for Tre to return to her parental custody. In the café scene between Furious and Reva, what would otherwise be a pro-feminist stance is rendered feminist backlash as Reva asserts that by raising his son, Furious has done nothing special, has done nothing that black mothers have not been doing for years. This comes only after Reva has shown that she cannot raise Tre herself, nor can any other woman in the film rear a son.

These images of black mothers would not be so damning if they were not so pervasive. These three images are very calculated and positioned in a masculine coming of age narrative, in a community of men, in opposition to the only father in the film. This community of men is in struggle for salvation and survival. Consequently, Furious, as the father, is a messianic figure, harkening salvation, bringing control and order back to the community. With Tre as the son and protagonist growing up in the mire of South Central Los Angeles, the salvation of the community is through the resurrection and preservation of this masculinity. Again, as in *House Party,* there is the instructional representation of the role model. In the case of *Boyz,* Tre is posited as the role model because he has a role model, his father Furious Styles. As a consequence, Tre is invested with the future of the filmic community.

## NEW BLACK CINEMA RECONSIDERED

In 1991 there were some nineteen films by black directors scheduled for release. By the end of 1991, at least twelve of these films were released with the backing of big Hollywood studios (Cole 1992). Clearly these films were popular and profitable, but the content and subject matter of these films, black people, black people's lives and cultural space and identity, were seemingly in contrast to Hollywood's racial traditions. As popular trends go, New Black Cinema was preceded by rap and hip-hop music, the popular image of the "endangered black man" and the sociological interest in drugs, crime and the inner city, all of which are portrayed by the media as a black dilemma (Jones 1991). The strategy of New Black Cinema was to recode the existing codings of blackness, informing the symbolic with the social and cultural sensibilities of black culture, Afrocentrism, and the everyday experiences of black people.

On the one hand, the issues of blackness, nationalism, and masculinity present in these early New Black Cinema films, in my reading, raise critical questions about the representations themselves; on the other hand, as Guerrero (1998) notes, these filmmakers in their mainstream, independent, and insurgent forms and tendencies expose and negotiate discriminatory practices in Hollywood (around marketing, promotion, and development of "black-themed" films) and, in doing so, engage and often explicitly provide a reading, a hermeneutic investigation, of American culture: as problematic as *School Daze, House Party,* and *Boyz N the Hood* are, they do present blackness and black masculinity as a site of interpretation, critique, and ethical engagement, as ongoing projects and cultural formations.

In the New Black Cinema films examined above, race as a discourse, especially as popular American discourse, functions in models of exceptionalism, talent and virtuosity, as these models are deployed for racial, social and political uplift (not surprisingly, most of these films are often described as masculine narratives). This New Black Cinema moment is an example of the early self-positions in West's new cultural politics of difference, and exclusive "talented tenth" grouping, a grouping which opened market and audience doors. Yet, there has been a marked shift; the issues and questions of racial representation have markedly changed. One can, on the one hand, argue that New Black Cinema has integrated and been assimilated into the American film machine (older filmmakers who have benefited like Michael Schultz and Bill Duke, and more recently Forrest Whitaker); on the other hand, black filmmakers are now the interpreters of whiteness. By this I mean that black cinema has, through the efforts of New Black Cinema, developed a market and audience, which reflect not only its success as a popular form, but also its critical interrogations and interpretations of blackness and race.

This latter aspect of black cinema as critical interrogation and interpretation is where New Black Cinema has shifted in emphasis. As mentioned in Chapter One, black cinema as a signifyin(g) practice which functions as a hermeneutic device allows a performative interplay between the cinematic apparatus, narrative structure and the historical and discursive constructions of race embedded in the use of the apparatus of cinema. It is this interplay among apparatus, narrative and history in which a hermeneutic shift has taken place, re-configuring the use and function of the "race" and gender rubric.

Let me clarify: two high profile national and media incidents reframed the discursivity of black masculinity in the 1990s: The Rodney King beating, the Simi Valley jury's acquittal of the police officers responsible and the subsequent protests and riots (1992); and the O.J. Simpson verdict (1995). With the Rodney King beating, verdict and riot, black masculinity is re-iterated in notions of aggression, submission, and criminality and simultaneously re-positioned within notions of collective and historical victimhood and denied and delayed state justice. The black masculine is violently removed from a liberal discourse of race pathology and re-inscribed in a Foucaultian notion of the state. The simultaneity of iteration and inscription, on the one hand, serves to universalize the black man as victim (in that the Rodney King beating is an incident of state control, of which everyone is a victim); on the other hand, the simultaneity of iteration and inscription serves to particularize the state's relationship to the black body (in that the black male body is the demonstrative body).

In the O.J. Simpson case, there is a greater sense of cultural betrayal. As an actor and entrepreneur, Simpson was an exemplar of the democratic ethos of celebrity; a model of the athletic masculine ideal; and an exemplar of integration and racial harmony. However, the trial for the murder of Nicole Brown Simpson and Ronald Goldman re-blackened, so to speak, his celebrity and masculinity: The black man is re-criminalized as the brute, the rapist, and the threat to white femininity and civility. With his acquittal, O.J. Simpson became a figure of "black" justice (especially in light of the initial Rodney King verdict); at the same time, he became a figure of liberal white injustice. By this I mean that Simpson valorized the American justice system of fair trail, while he vilified the American dream and the American ideal of integration.

The question becomes, what is the impact of these ambiguous, discursive black masculinities in the realm of representation, mass media and entertainment? These two figures, Rodney King and O.J. Simpson—the quotidian and the celebrity, the everyday and the iconic—become a split image fused in the cultural imaginary as the limit and horizon of the representation of black masculinity.[12] It is the horizon of the representation of black masculinity because it is ambiguous, rendering the representation of black masculinity as inassimilable to stereotype and stereotypic representation; the split image is the limit of the representation of black masculinity because in its ambiguity the split image reveals the disavowed contradictions of American class and racial ideals, a productive and profitable disavowal, indeed the disavowal of entertainment itself.

The mediations of this split image have been subtle, partially through the co-optation and absorption of black-themed narratives and characters into popular culture as economically viable entertainment (films and especially hip-hop inflected films which use rap artists as actors) and partially through the movement of black filmmakers into more mainstream projects.[13] In the post-Rodney King/Simpson verdict era, the standardized hood film, unable to engage the conflicts and contradictions of the 1990s black masculine, fell into redundancy similar to Blaxploitation. At the same time, there were "applications" similar to those of Blaxploitation (the application of blackness to standard, tried and true narratives) in films like *Tales from the Hood* (1995) and *Vampire in Brooklyn* (1995), exploring race and horror. However, films that confronted race more historically, critically and confrontationally in the established masculine narrative mode of New Black Cinema failed at the box office.[14]

In partial recognition of the shifting significations of race and masculinity, Guerrero (1998) notes that the racial climate and popular audience mood immediately following the O.J. Simpson verdict contributed to the box office failure of two films specifically, *Devil in a Blue Dress* (1995) and *Strange Days* (1995) (349). It is my contention that, yes, on that October weekend in 1995, the majority American audience was unwilling to confront a film like *Devil* or *Strange Days* because of their emphasis on race, but also I contend that black cinema, in its New Black Cinema permutation, can no longer support the masculine narratives of a film like *Devil* because of the conflicting split imagery of media black masculinity. In other words, the prototypical, recuperative imagery of black men in the early films of New Black Cinema are no longer viable representations because of their uncomplicated, simplistically redemptive discursivity.

Two things have happened: First, New Black Cinema has succeeded in changing the face of American cinema in that black-themed films, black male characters, and black male stars have multiplied and done so with economic and industrial success.[15] Second, in the expansion of market and audience, there are greater demands on the black film. With the ambiguity of the black male and the black male narrative, there is necessarily a change in subject matter, different themes of racialized subject formations, different thematic contexts for the black male. This has entailed a move away from the masculine, urban centered narrative of the initial outpouring of New Black Cinema[16] to the decidedly Post New Black Cinema focus on family (both urban and rural), the black middle class, and female centered narrative and to the Post New Black Cinema shift in the signifying practices of race and black cinema. With the second significatory component, I mean to suggest that blackness is inscribed in recent films in a more aesthetic manner as a way of looking, as a way of being, as opposed to the black character or *mise-en-scène* of blackness determining and defining the films of New Black Cinema. In the first instance and the broadening of narratives, I refer to films like *Soul Food, Down in the Delta, Eve's Bayou, Friday, The Brothers, Kingdom Come, Set It Off,* and *Waiting to Exhale,* to name a few. In the second instance, I refer to films like *Summer of Sam* and the more recent *From Hell* in which blackness is rendered as a transgeneric hermeneutic device which provides an interpretation of whiteness in narratives about white men.

To better understand the New to the Post New, I return to the discussion the Du Bosian gift. New Black Cinema emerges from a historic and political awareness of double consciousness in that the initial project is a recoding of blackness and black masculinity, exposing a hypocrisy in representation. In doing so, New Black Cinema reveals an incompleteness in the social formations of black men, a sub-personhood in the representation of black masculinity, positing itself as criticism and critical practice as cultural production. With the shift to Post New Black Cinema and the ambiguity of black masculinity as the signifier of race, there is a Foucaultian "work on the self" and emphasis on blackness and black cultural production and civil responsibility in re-defining, expanding, and critiquing blackness from the incompleteness of black masculine sup-personhood.

# Chapter Five
# "Untitled": D'Angelo and the Visualization of the Black Male Body

The "Untitled" of this essay signifies not only on the title of D'Angelo's popular song, but also on the un-titling of masculinity that D'Angelo signifies through his discursive play with masculinity and blackness and through the visualization of the black male body. As such, this essay is approaching three things: one is a look at the text and the black male body and another is a look at the spectatorial practices that this text engenders. Finally, in consideration of the text and spectatorial practices, I approach the question of gender ethics or ethical gender constructs as they are provoked by the visual medium of music video. For the first part, I examine the African American male body, its pop cultural contingencies and visualization, in one recent visual text, D'Angelo's video for "Untitled (How does it feel?)"(Paul Hunter 1999).This text is noted not only for the nudity but also for the visualization of the black male body as an erotic object. For the second part, spectatorship provides an opportunity to foreground the relationship between the reader/viewer and the text and the critical response embodied. Finally, for the third part, ethical questions are raised in the particularity of the object of music video itself.

Because of the text, its formal strategies, and its dialogic construction and intertextual referentiality, I begin by situating it in a more encompassing discourse of visual culture. This discussion is formed in an understanding of music video as a discrete form and artifact; at the same time, there is the secondary understanding that this specific video is in visual exchange with photography. The video is arguably part of the broader category of visual culture. By visual culture, I rely on Nicholas Mirzoeff's (1999) formulation of visual culture " . . . [as] concerned with visual events in which information, meaning or pleasure is sought by the consumer in an interface with visual technology" (3). Visual culture, then, emphasizes not only the object—what is looked at—but also the technology and the consumption of that object at the level of the viewer and at the level of the object's relationship to other objects as objects that are seen, as objects that are visualized. Situating D'Angelo's video within the broader discourse of visual culture provides an opportunity for an exploration of the present/absent medium, photography, in the video. In this instance, I follow Mirzoeff in understanding that the "task" of visual culture is to discern the complex relations between and among images (7).

## D'ANGELO AND POST-SOUL

Let's begin with D'Angelo, some background and justification for discussion of him. D'Angelo, the lyricist, musician, singer and performer, first appeared on the music scene in 1995 with the very successful album, *Brown Sugar.* Much of his public image is constructed around his relationship to music, black male musicians (Prince, Hendrix, and Marvin Gaye, especially) and spirituality (his southern, rural Pentecostal upbringing) and sexuality. These aspects of his image are demonstrated in, for example, the "reports" of his reading Marvin Gaye's autobiography and its importance to his identity and music; his discussion of visions and dreams during the making of the album, *Voodoo;* and more recently, his spiritual recounting of the birth of his son (Hampton 2000, 106; and Questlove 1999, np).

D'Angelo is categorically a music auteur, having more control of his career, musical and lyrical endeavors, and production. As an auteur, there are expressive elements of style and content in his music which function as a signature, personal expression, and signs of individual authorship.[1] Furthermore as an auteur, D'Angelo's musical ethos is one of, on the one hand, an iconoclastic and rebellious funk ethic in which there is a musical blending and experimentation among rock, soul and rhythm and blues and the demonstrated coalition of musical styles through the use of collectives and artist collaboration. Also, there is in funk a configuration of blackness as fluid and ambiguous and, to some extent, in opposition to traditional fixed notions of blackness and the proprieties of blackness. D'Angelo identifies this blackness as the "dirt," as a willingness to be messy in blending, citing, referencing and incorporating other musical traditions (Questlove, np). In this instance, D'Angelo is something of a "funk band leader" in the tradition of Jimi Hendrix, Prince, Sly Stone, and George Clinton. On the other hand, D'Angelo is noted as a soul singer, primarily because of his musical arrangements, lyrics (love and sex), his vocal performance in falsetto, and "soul intertextuality" (as his vocal performances reference, tribute and sample crooners before him like Otis Redding, Marvin Gaye, and Smokey Robinson; and his musical arrangements and instrumentation provide contemporary, updated versions of soul music's orchestration, lyrics and vocal arrangements, at the same time that they blend more contemporary musical codes like drum programming, sampling and guest mcees).

However, on a more culturally symbolic plane, as opposed to the strictly formal fields of funk and soul music, D'Angelo is arguably post-soul. Nelson George configures post-soul as a contemporary condition of black culture, a condition that "hinges on the way two fringe movements, hip hop and black film, came up from the underground, . . . reflect[ing] the unending debate over authenticity, co-optation, and redefinition that desegregation's new opportunities and contradiction intensified" (George 1992, 6). Post-soul, similar to Cornel West's new cultural politics of difference, marks a re-territorialization of the cultural fields of production and consumption. The descriptor "post-soul" describes a cultural current which not only destabilizes fixed notions of racial and gendered identities, but also opens and explores new consumer markets, creating audiences and producing sedimented and intertextual objects for entertainment consumption.

D'Angelo is situated in the post-soul era as a singer, songwriter, and performer very in tune to the four points on soul's discursive compass: gender, sexuality, spirituality, and blackness. This is evident in two aspects of his persona. First in reference to gender and blackness, his attendance to image follows a pattern of change in appearance with the promotion for *Brown Sugar,* his first album, to *Voodoo,* his second. Photographs and videos for *Brown Sugar* present D'Angelo as a contemporary, urban black male. In his promotional photographs for the first album, he is dressed as a typical hip-hopper, the oversized clothes, leather bomber, cornrows and antagonistic cool pose. Though his music is not now, nor was it then, identifiably hip-hop or rap inspired, it is hip-hop inflected. As a marketing strategy, the use of hip-hop fashion and gesture target a readily available and lucrative music audience and market and indicates and references hip-hop as a visual and fashion trend and sensibility, as well as a musical idiom. Hip-hop fashion, furthermore, has the dual strategy of aggression and containment. By this I mean that with men the multilayered, oversized clothing, the bandanas, and the baggy pants revealing boxers are fashionably aggressive in their appropriation of "street" and *couture,* celebrating the accoutrement of prison and gang culture with the sophistication and timeliness of *prêt-a-porter.* At the same time, men's hip-hop fashion is containment, through concealment, of the body. The layeredness of the attire controls corporeal exposure. The resulting image is one of an aggressive, combative, urbane, tightly held masculinity.

This is in stark contrast to the cover of and promotionals for *Voodoo,* the second album. Here, D'Angelo is always revealed shirtless, showing his tattoos and honed musculature. This D'Angelo image is arguably part of a national trend, emerging in the late 90s, which offered more sensual, yet scintillating, exposure of the male body in popular media.[2] Perhaps, in response to the late 80s and early 90s popularization in film and fashion of the drag queen and queer boy aesthetic, the late 90s counter image is constructed as "counter" in the objectifying exposure of the male body. This counter image is suggestive of greater awareness to the physical form and is a stabilizing gender image in that these images are resolutely heterosexual, reclaiming straight masculinity within the trend of the sensitive man willing to expose himself.[3] Again, D'Angelo's imagery is in tune to his market and does not stray from the current of popular male representation. His image only adjusts the representation to hip-hop inflected soul, presenting the ideal as one within blackness and through signifiers of blackness.[4]

The second aspect of D'Angelo's persona that reveals its soul discursivity is his overt musical and historical alignment with soul music as a signifier of sexuality and spirituality. "Untitled (How does it feel?)," which is relatively simple lyrically, is transformed through the vocal performance and the promotional construction of *Voodoo,* the album, as a spiritual journey.[5] In this discursive and promotional framework, "How does it feel," which in a hip-hop or rock performance would invoke violence and misogyny as penetration, instead invokes an existential crisis and spiritual question of sexual difference.[6] In other words, through performance and discourse, D'Angelo raises the question of "How does it feel" from the position of the all-knowing masculine subject, as a question of an absence of knowledge, and as such in the gendered dynamics of the utterance and spiritual quest, the question becomes a revelation of gender and sexual difference and an admission and quest for knowledge in that difference. Though visually, and to some extent musically, inflected in the urbane, hard-edged masculinity of hip-hop and rap, the fluid expression and interrogation of sexuality and spirituality align D'Angelo more with the soul music form of soul searching, sexual spirituality, and romantic love, like that found in Marvin Gaye's "Sexual Healing" or Al Green's "Simply Beautiful" or "Belle."

## AUSTERITY, DIALOG AND FETISHISM

As far as music videos go, the video for "How does it feel?" is an austere piece, consisting of D'Angelo, seemingly on a pedestal, naked, singing. However, the austerity of the video renders the visualization of the song as one more within a photographic tradition than a video one. By this I mean that the sparseness of the *mise-en-scène,* the studied use of the close-up and lighting, the 360° longtake, the attention to the body, the segmentation of the body, etc., simultaneously renders the music video to be, formally, a study, a male nude study.

As a study, D'Angelo's body is situated in two separate photographic traditions/histories, one of the black male nude as the sign of hypersexuality, criminality, and, in pornography, the sign of a preference or sexual proclivity; and the other tradition, following the formal aspirations of the video, situates the body in a tradition of the fine arts nude in which the male nude, its form and iconography represents ideals of beauty, the universal ideals of reason and masculinity and whiteness. Furthermore, in the second fine arts photographic tradition, the video is in a dialog with two photographic discursive trajectories: first the video mimics Robert Mapplethorpe's (1988 and 1986) formalist photography, in which there is the insertion of the black body into the male nude tradition, framing the body in abstract, objectified codes of beauty; and second, the video borrows from the work of Geoffrey Holder (1986), in which the black male body is inserted into the same discourse of ideal beauty, without the emphasis on the formal properties of the photographic medium and with a greater emphasis on the celebration of the form of the male body.

Published before Mapplethorpe's work, and perhaps languishing in a dearth of criticism because of it, Holder's *Adam* is a traditional study of the male nude emphasizing the architecture of the male body, the musculature and contours of the body as it is defined as male. The photographs in *Adam* are tightly framed shots of men dancing or in dance poses. There are no faces, frontal nudity or individual expressions of the models; the models are not identified by name. The photographs in high contrast black and white and closely cropped framing accent the musculature of the bodies as the object of study. Furthermore, the accompanying text narrativizes the ordering of the photographs as a creation myth, or in Holder's description as "an exploration of birth, the birth of the first man, the birth of us all."

The imposed narrative *telos* of birth aids in rendering the collection picturesque, vividly expressive of the emergence of form. There is, on the other hand, a de-emphasis on race, a de-emphasis on the fact that all of his subjects are black men. The use of high contrast black and white reveals the subjects of the photographs to be black men; however, there is no visual discursivity of race which objectifies the men in blackness. In other words, the use of the models in dance poses, the close cropping of the photographs to study musculature, curvature and contour, and the lack of frontal nudity provide the photographs with an aesthetic frame that engender the black body as the universal ideal male body.

In contrast, Mapplethorpe steers the viewer in another discursive direction, one which is predicated upon race (as the title, *Black Male,* suggests) as a signifier of difference, both racial and sexual. Granted, Mapplethorpe's aesthetic project is indeed quite different from that of Holder. Were it not for the universal ideal of masculinity, and its accompanying racial ideal, and the use of black men in the expression of these ideals, one would find no mutual point of reference between these two photographers' work. Whereas Holder's work may be described as picturesque, expressively narrativizing masculine ideals through creation, Mapplethorpe's work may be described as statuesque, engaging the formal aspects of photography through lighting and through the reproduction of sculptural poses. The men's bodies are reproduced as detailed photographic reproductions of statues in a careful display of light, pose and posture.

As Kobena Mercer suggests, the photographs of black men in Mapplethorpe's work provide "perspectives, vantage points and 'takes'" on black men (Mercer 1994, 174). The nudes are varying in their degree of explicitness, varying from poses on pedestals to frontal nudity, framing the penis as portrait. Mercer continues to note: " . . . Mapplethorpe appropriates elements of commonplace racial stereotypes in order to regulate, organize, prop up and *fix* the process of erotic/aesthetic objectification in which the black man's flesh becomes burdened with the task of symbolizing the transgressive fantasies and desires of the white gay male subject" (176). This reading is suggestive of one aesthetic appropriation of the visual codes of the black male body. This reading, furthermore, frames the "appropriation of the black male body" within the concept of fetishism.

Mercer's use of fetishism engages both the Freudian, psychoanalytic concept and the Marxist concept of commodity fetishism—both sexual and economic fetishization—leading him to conclude that the black men in Mapplethorpe's work (a conclusion which can be extended to some degree to Holder's) undergo an "erasure of any social interference" (177). In other words, there is an effacement of the disparate social and racial relations between the well known artist and the unknown, and often unidentified, black models. Mercer continues to suggest that the intersecting discourses of the fetish "super impos[e] two ways of seeing—the nude which eroticizes the act of looking, and the stereotype which imposes fixity," leading to ambivalence in reading and producing male images (177–178).[7] Mercer's use of fetishism and ambivalence is closer in meaning and concept to Anne McClintock's, which conceptualizes the fetish and fetishism as conflict and contradiction and historicizes the fetish and fetishism as a point of intersection among Enlightenment anthropology of man, Marxism, and psychoanalysis; indeed, for McClintock, fetishism is the "historical enactment of ambiguity itself":

. . . fetishes can be seen as the displacement onto an object (or person) of contradictions that the individual cannot resolve at a personal level. These contradictions may originate as social contradictions but are lived with profound intensity in the imagination and the flesh. The fetish thus stands at the cross-roads of psychoanalysis and social history, inhabiting the threshold of both personal and historical memory. The fetish marks a crisis in social meaning as the embodiment of an impossible irresolution. The contradiction is displaced onto and embodied in the fetish object, which is thus destined to recur with compulsive repetition. Hence the apparent power of the fetish to enchant the fetishist. By displacing power onto the fetish, then manipulating the fetish, the individual gains symbolic control over what might otherwise be terrifying ambiguities (McClintock 1994, 89).[8]

Holder and Mapplethorpe's photography as sites of ambivalence and fetishism as a concept of ambivalence, ambiguity and conflict and contradiction provide insight into the D'Angelo video. Indeed, it is this productive point of ambivalence at which we find fetishism and D'Angelo's video; for fetishism, in Mercer and McClintock's uses, allows for a broader use of the concept, beyond a phallocentric, psychoanalytic use and deterministic commodity fetishist use, to encompass a broader, more expressive concept of self-fetishism in the video.

Self-fetishism, in this instance, is the contradictory moment of fetishism in the commodity form of the music video. Fetishism is conceptualized in the desire to see the naked body, the naked black body, the objectification of the body of D'Angelo the musician/video artist, and in the dialogic exchange between the music video and photography. The "self" aspect emerges in the projection of the self through the discourse of the artist and artistic genius inherent in D'Angelo as lyricist and musician. Let me elaborate by returning to the video.

As mentioned before, the video for "How does it feel" is quite austere: a slow, 360° longtake of D'Angelo, suspended and naked, singing, against a black backdrop. The video begins with an extreme close up, left pan across the back of D'Angelo's head, lingering on the details of his cornrows. D'Angelo's position on a turntable pedestal gives the illusion of suspension and of a mobile camera. As the pedestal turns, still in extreme close up, D'Angelo's eyes, mouth, and face are revealed. The frontal face shot is followed by a vertical tilt down and a zoom-out to a close up of his head and shoulders, followed by a second zoom to a medium shot revealing his face, shoulders, and upper torso. The video continues as a series of zooms toward and away from the focal points of D'Angelo's crucifix and his navel. The dénouement sequence proceeds from a medium long shot of D'Angelo's shoulder down to his buttocks in profile, concluding with a medium shot from his waist up, his arms extended. The video ends with a close up of D'Angelo's face, with a direct address to the camera.

The video is a rich exchange of photographic, video, and performance codes. Mercer, again in his discussion of Mapplethorpe, identifies three photographic codes guiding male nudes in general and Mapplethorpe in particular: 1). the sculptural code, concerning the posing and posture of the body; 2). the portraiture code, concerning the concentration on the face; and 3). the lighting and framing code, fragmenting the body into textured formal abstractions (Mercer 178). When considering these photographic codes as they are dialogically embedded in the video, there are three significant video codes at play: 1). the spatial code, concerning the distance between the camera and the object and camera movement toward and away from and around the object and the framing of the object: this is done with the use of the zoom, close up, medium close up and medium long shot framing and with the use of tracking, circular camera movement, and pans and tilts; 2). the temporal code, concerning the duration of the image and the use of the longtake; and 3). the musical code, concerning the deployment of sound not only for the purpose of narration, explanation and dialog (as in a more narrative filmic coding and use of sound), but also for the accompaniment and compliment, which renders the image (photographic and video) as illustration of music, lyrics and sound. The spatial code is an adaptation and extension to video of the sculptural, lighting, and portraiture codes of photography identified by Mercer, giving the photographic quality of the image video discursivity, depth of space and perspective in space and movement. The temporal and music codes are properly video codes, rendering the photographic quality of the image "extended play," so to speak. In other words, the temporal and music codes alter the photographic quality of the image.

The photographic and video codes provide an aesthetic and social framework for understanding the performance. The performance itself is defined by three specific performance codes: 1). the gestural codes, concerning the use of the body and gesture: the D'Angelo video is gesturally coded in the use of his eyes, hand and arm gestures, upper body motion, and the sensual gesturing of licking his lips; 2). vocal codes, concerning the soul musical tradition encoded in his vocal performance, registered in the lyrics of the song and in the use of the falsetto as a pleading question; and 3). codes of the performative visual medium, in this case music video, which can be sub-divided into secondary spatial codes and secondary temporal codes (secondary to the spatial and temporal video codes). The video camera codes enable a specifically video performance. These codes are marked by expressive camera use: the use of rapid edits, obscure camera angles, the mobile camera, and close on the face, mouth, and hands: The camera often attends to performative body movement. The secondary temporal codes circumscribe the performance and the presentation of the performance in that the song, the version of the song (re-mix, album version, radio edit, etc.) determines the duration of the performance, scripts the performance, so to speak.

As for the performance itself, austerity reproduces austerity: the performance is confined to the limited space of the revolving pedestal and is comprised of gestures of external affection and attention, extended arms and beckoning hands; gestures of interiority, down cast eyes, closed eyes, eyes cast away from the camera; gestures of self-affection and self-eroticism, caressing himself and licking his lips; and gestures of direct address as seen in his eye contact with the camera and audience. This performance is further eroticized by the codes of video performance, mentioned earlier. By this I mean that the camera movement, the pans and tilts, attends to the movement of D'Angelo's arms, his hands, the rise and fall of his abdomen, the movement of sweat, at the same time that the camera framing, the use of the zoom in and out, attends to the arc of the song, the crescendos and decrescendos of the music and lyrics.

In other words, D'Angelo's performance of the song is, as expected of music video, a performance for the camera and a performance with an implied audience beyond the camera. Furthermore, D'Angelo's performance is a performance of eroticism and sensuality as the song "How does it feel" requires in the performance of it, that the performer project erotic and sensual engagement. In addition, the medium of video, through the manipulation of form and technique, on the one hand, *performs* photography, reproduces a photographic aesthetic and discourse around D'Angelo's body, the black male body, and the male body ideal; and on the other hand, through camera movement and framing, the music video performs as an apparatus of entertainment and visual pleasure across D'Angelo's body, presenting a visualization of discursive blackness, of the black male body as a self-objectifying erotic object.

## WHAT DOES IT LOOK LIKE?

At this point I want to shift the discussion to spectatorship and "How does it feel." It is important to examine the particularity of the object, of the music video form. By this I mean to examine the video not only in its distinctiveness as a D'Angelo video, but also the form, of music video as a distinct form, as distinct in and of itself. In order to do this I draw on the work of Ian Heywood and the particularity of art, which he defines as follows:

> By particularity I mean that pieces are not only unique things but that their uniqueness is part of their artistic value. The fact that there is only one painting or sculpture 'like this' does not in itself greatly matter, at least artistically. But the precise *ways* in which a painting or sculpture is itself, and the efforts the artist has gone to in order to make its visible or sensible qualities specific, matter crucially (Heywood 1999, 198–217).

For, the particularity of art leads to a particularity in perception, or as Heywood continues:

> . . . the idea of achieved particularity in a work of art connects it with a certain view of individual human beings, that they too may, perhaps should, aim at individuation or self-realisation. It is not enough simply to 'be oneself,' rather the individual is called upon, has a responsibility, to realize his or her potential for individuality in such a way that the result is not only difference in the sense of absolute uniqueness but also difference as something significance, both in itself and for others (Heywood 199)

Particularity and its perception are important because the ethical dimension in the dyad confronts practical matters and practical reason. As Heywood notes, practical matters are "mutable, indeterminate and indefinable, and . . . unique to some specific case" (Heywood 206). The uniqueness of the intended object and intentionality of practical reason are applicable to the contingencies of subjective interrogations of race present in artworks and performance and the trajectory of the individuation of self-realization in response to and viewership of the artwork. Furthermore, self-realization presupposes incompleteness, in this case ethical incompleteness.[9] The shift to particularity here in my discussion is strategic as an elevation of music video to an art form and as an address to the question of spectatorship and the individuality that "How does it feel" inspires in viewing.

In understanding music video as an artistic form and in its particularity, we must understand it as an intertextual medium and a highly commodified, if not hyper-commodified object. Music video, as a discrete artistic object, transverses the media of music, film, television, and video. As a consumer product in its commodity form, music video is a promotional tool of radio, the music industry, and television. In order to raise the question of spectatorship, it is necessary to examine music video in all its interrelations as artistic expression and consumer product. First, music video is primarily a televisual form, adhering to temporal constraints of television (the length of the video is usually three to five minutes), content and subject-matter constraints and the target audience/slotted programming constraints. Second, music video is a "mini-film" form often drawing on the musical film genre form and employing narrative strategies and continuity editing style established by film (though definitely not dependent on film; and certainly at this stage in development as a popular medium, music video is in rich exchange with and influencing film). Third, as a musical form, music video is a re-presentation of the song, often employing different versions, edits, or different directors. As a commodity form, music video is primarily promotional, functioning as advertising for the musical artist and record label. For example, as well as a discrete "text," the video for "How does it feel," is a re-presentation of the song as part of a marketing strategy, a promotion of the song and artist, giving the song "airplay" in the same manner as radio airplay. In this regard music video is similar to a television commercial.

Considering the relationship between media and market, music video is best seen in its particularity as a genre of television. In this way, music video is seen as a form similar to a television series, with programming constraints, slots and target audience, or seen as a television commercial, with the primary objective of marketing and selling a product. The genricity of music video, its discrete formation as a "kind of television," lies in its programming, its specificity to video channels and networks. This aspect of programming distinguishes music video from commercials and solely functioning as advertising, and aligns it with other televisual, generic narrative forms such as series and soap operas. As a genre, it is the relation to film and music that distinguishes music video from other television genres. Unlike other television genres, genres which use music as accompaniment, music video is motivated by music, lyrics and performer (not performance or narrative, though the video may be narrative): re-presentation of the song as a televisually consumerable product is the motivation for music video's generic formation.

As a televisual, filmic and generic form, music video raises different questions of spectatorship. Generically, music video, first and foremost, raises the question of audience expectation, as audience is inscribed in intention, convention and form. This is a twofold expectation: First, in the form of televisual genre; and second, in the form of musical genre (soul, rock, punk, pop, etc). Generic expectation is generated also in television programming. With, for example, MTV (Music Television), the genre or kind of song (rap, rock, romantic, metal, etc.) has specific time slots, specific times at which a particular kind of song will appear. As for the televisual expectation of music video, the form provides a "mini-movie," visualizing a song as entertainment, as a text which can be "read" in the confines of the home and the medium of television. As such, the music video is required to present succinctly and visually the lyrics of the song, dramatized, narrativized or performed in a concert or non-narrative performance which conveys the lyrics and music and showcases the performer.

Filmically, as mentioned earlier, music video draws on filmic conventions of continuity editing. The use of these conventions suture the viewer into the video, as the video form presents itself in familiarity, in the conventional apparatus of continuity. Much has been said about the conventions of film and spectatorship. Of concern to the present discussion here is Laura Mulvey's (1989) "Visual Pleasure and Narrative Cinema" and the concept of the gaze. For Mulvey, psychoanalysis offers an explanation for the structure of narrative around scopophilia and masculine identification. As a construction of power, identification and patriarchy, the gaze is masculine, possessing pleasure in looking, projecting fantasies onto its object. What is the object of the gaze is feminine, the passive, static receiver of action, that which is possessed by the gaze. As the gaze and its stand-in (usually the male protagonist/looker) are cinematically and psychically constructed, there is an active/passive split between the gaze and the object, between the narrative and spectacle, between man and woman: The gaze and the object are structured along the lines of sexual difference. The implications of the gaze for spectatorship suggest that the spectator of classic narrative cinema is always male, and heterosexual. The D'Angelo video offers an opportunity for disruption in that in a filmic convention D'Angelo is feminized, objectified, and rendered wholly as spectacle.

However, even though the cinematic conventions of continuity editing often reproduce scenes of voyeurism, positioning the spectator's gaze as one of masculine power over the image of woman or the feminized other and are at work in the televisual, television as a medium presupposes different spectatorial relations than the cinematic. The conditions of television consumption are guided by the specificity of the medium. Television is a far more intimate medium than film, more domestic, more private. Television engenders a different organization of time: The continuous follow of television: "It's always on"; and the temporal system programming shows for the viewer: Primetime, Saturday morning programming, daytime programming, etc. There is a conflation of time and genre/content. Television, also in the American context, has the presence of ruptures and breaks as part of its visuality and visual flow of information because of commercial advertising.

Because of its mode of consumption and compartmentalized, continuous, yet disrupted visuality, John Ellis suggests that the television has a "glance," a look without the power of the gaze, as opposed to the cinematic gaze (Ellis 1982, 137–139). The television viewer is more in control of the look, but as an experience of intimacy and privacy, and of collectivity and community. Baudrillard, in a more hyperbolic postmodernist mode, suggests that the visuality of television is the collapse of all opposition: "The whole traditional mode of causality is brought into question: the perspective, deterministic mode, the 'active,' critical mode, the analytical mode—the distinction between cause and effect, between active and passive, between subject and object, between ends and means" (Baudrillard 1983, 55). For Baudrillard, this collapse leads to simulation, "where the distinction between poles can no longer be maintained" (57). For the purpose here it is important to note that the collapse that becomes simulation, that produces the "glance" as opposed to the gaze, also implies a collapse of sexual difference in spectatorship.

Yet Lynne Joyrich notes this collapse and dissolution of difference in Ellis and Baudrillard is false in that they simply reconfigure spectators, in the absence of masculine difference, as feminized, as rendered feminine in television consumption. Joyrich continues to argue that television is left in an odd gender conflict resulting in the construction of hypermasculinity: " . . . television as a whole exists in an odd tension, balanced between the modern and the postmodern . . . and between culturally constituted notions of the feminine and the masculine. . . . This places television in a curious bind—a situation perhaps most evident in many prime-time programs which, in order to be 'culturally' respectable and appeal to male viewers, attempt to elevate the infantile and deny the feminine conventionally associated with television. . . . A common strategy of television is thus to construct a violent hypermasculinity—an excess of 'maleness' that acts as a shield" (Joyrich 1990, 156–172).

As a hypermasculine display of video soul and an anthem of heterosexual romantic love, the intended audience for "Untitled," the viewer in text, is arguably female. However, as a televisual form, one can arguably say that the intended audience, the viewer in the text can only be that—an intended audience, a discursively and lyrically constructed viewer. In other words, though the video may have a gender specific, target audience, the video form, as a televisual and, in this case, an intertextual, dialogic form, opens the spectatorial door, so to speak, providing a point of entry for a number of spectator/discursive subject positions: There is the heterosexual female spectator sutured into the text as target; and there are the spectatorial others, who enter the viewer position through entertainment, eroticism and homoeroticism, and hypermasculinity.

This assessment of the television text and spectatorship could damn any consideration of the music video for "How does it feel" as a throw away pop form, as an open text and as a construction of hypermasculinity, as reactive and recuperative visualization. Indeed, the video is a representation of reactive and recuperative hypermasculinity; "How does it feel" is hypermasculine—it is so in citation, repetition, and re-iteration. By this I mean that the discursive strategy of dialog with photography and blackness in the video and the use of music video as the means of conducting the dialog embody a performative and textual instance of signifyin(g). The particularity of the music video and its ensuing spectatorial practices which, as Joyrich suggests, engage the viewer in re-compensatory images and imaginings of masculinity and gendered indentificatory positioning—in this case "How does it feel" and the significatory practices in regards to the fetishized image of black masculinity—inspires a responsibility in the viewer: The responsibility of the perception of particularity.

In other words, the display of D'Angelo citing hypermasculinity, racialized and objectified masculinity, the embrace of this masculinity, and the re-articulation of it as lack, doubt, difference, and incommensurability reveal the project of a critical engagement with masculinity, race, and their negative discursivity. Furthermore, as the particularity of the video and music video specifically are discernable, the viewer, in perceiving the particular, has an ethical priority, a priority to individuation and self-realization (Heywood 205). This ethical priority and the formation of it as self-realization imply an ethical incompleteness, which appears as an instanciation of practical reason with attention to practical matters. Practical matters are contingent, mutable indeterminate, specific and unpredictable. In the case of "How does it feel," questions of race and racialized gender are rendered as practical questions of self and desire and given moral valuations as ethical incompleteness and self-realization in the dynamics of particularity and the perception of particularity.

# Conclusion

The project as outlined in the introduction has been to put three sets of "boys" in conversation with each other in an effort to reveal and contemplate ethical questions of masculinity and race, as masculinity and race constitute forms of knowledge, perception, and modes of understanding. Ethics is understood in two forms. The first notion of ethics is in the Enlightenment thinking of Immanuel Kant and the universalizing category of the person. In this instance, ethics is rooted in the concepts of duty, responsibility and respect for humanity as an end in itself. The project here has been to interrogate the sedimentary assumptions of race in this philosophical tradition of ethics. The assumptions in this tradition of ethics presuppose racialized others as sub-persons, as less than ideal human subjects. Furthermore, the category of the sub-person demarcates the moral and ethical possibilities of racialized others. In other words, sub-personhood, as a category of person, delineates the possibilities of moral standing and agency.

The second understanding of ethics is through Foucault and the care of the self as a practice of ethical subject formation. With this notion of ethics, there is the idea of ethics as a practice, a way of life and a way of being. Indeed, this notion of ethics is implicitly used to read and interrogate the more philosophical, Enlightenment version of ethics. By placing emphasis on the self, technologies of the self, and constructions of the self, the Foucaultian care of the self has allowed for the examination of cultural production, filmmaking, celebrity discourse and performance as criticism and ethical practice. This engagement with ethics is a "relativizing of the discipline's traditional hierarchies of importance and centrality," as described by Mills (1998), and in order to do this relativizing, there has been an elaboration of race and gender as *habitus* and performativity. As such, race and gender are rendered as contingent, experiential, and performative, as opposed to essential or biological social forms—hence the notion of "boys" as boys, boyz, and bois.

I argue that black masculinity is fully discursive and performative. Contemporary black masculinity, as well as black femininity and blackness as a racial signifier, is embedded in a liberal discourse of pathology and victimhood, cultural failure and social dysfunction. At the same time, black masculinity specifically is defined in the more vernacular discourse of performativity as cool pose, as a performative response to rhetorical and discursive pronouncements *about* black masculinity. It is worth noting that cool pose and the racial performativity that it embodies also engender an ethical dilemma with reference to notions of standards of gender, the construction of these standards, and the implicit racialism in these constructions.

I continue further to elaborate cool pose as racial performativity and racial performativity as a form of signigfyin(g), as a form of appropriation and critical redress of discourse. I extend this discussion of racial performativity from the corporeal cool pose to the cultural production arena of cinema and black film, arguing that the signifyin(g) which takes from as racial performativity provides an understanding of the dynamic operations of black film as a practice and hermeneutic device. It is through racial performativity and black cinema, celebrity, performance and cultural production I elaborate an ethics of gender.

Sidney Poitier figures as a primary site of the articulation of gender as an ethical construct. Autobiography becomes a technology of the self in Poitier's self-fashioning and self-restoration of himself as celebrity, intellectual and Race Man. During the re-invention of himself, Poitier offers critique of being the representative black, of being the racial exemplar; he answers critiques of his image, politics and racial authenticity. Furthermore, Poitier's negotiation of responsibility to himself and community brings to light the contingencies of race, racial pride, and gender. Poitier, through autobiographical self-invention, fashions himself as a Race Man, as a figure of masculine responsibility to family and community. At the same time, through his self-insertion into the traditions of star autobiography and African American autobiography, there is a concerted effort which, on the one hand, demonstrates the universality of the possibility of celebrity and the ascent to Race Man and, on the other, demonstrates the humanity and personhood of African Americans. Poitier's discursive exemplarity posits the acquisition of a unified masculine identity as an ethical commitment to self and community. That this exemplarity is established within responsibility, family and the democratic ethos of stardom further establishes Poitier's star status as an arrival of a "boy," in the ideal sense, proof of his status within the masculine ideal;

indeed, Poitier's arrival signals a critique of the "boy" status, foregrounding questions of what is "ideal," what is rendered ideal.

However, Poitier's boy is but one in an array of possibilities, perhaps the pinnacle, but by no means the limit. His arrival and integration into the conception of the standard boy is fraught with diverse and counter imagery. Poitier's integrated boy image is counter to boyz, a discursive boy that gives privilege to the racialized, particular significations of black masculinity. The discussion of Jim Brown and Blaxploitation attends to the emergence of boyz in the Blaxploitation/black community debate about class, quality, and authenticity. The early Jim Brown imagery is inserted in the array of filmic masculinities; however, Brown is decidedly different from Poitier. Brown's image is a celebration of the masculine form, sexual prowess, and aggression, a return to nature of sorts. As opposed to an ascent to Race Man, Brown's imagery is a reconciliation of the iconic and the quotidian; Brown becomes exemplary, not of humanity or masculinity of the Race Man, but of the Black Man as a figure of the particularity of man. Whereas the trajectory of Poitier's boys and Race Man ultimately lead to a universal image of the black man as categorically "a man," Brown's boyz, though integrated into masculine difference, lead to a pluralism celebrating the difference of black masculinity as a trope of authenticity that Poitier's imagery cannot signify.

It is this particularity of boyz that is narrativized in Blaxploitation as authentic. However, unlike Jim Brown, the masculinity of Blaxploitation is inassimilable because of its rendering visible of whiteness as oppression. Let me clarify: Poitier's masculine identity is more integrated as equality and universalism, though critical of masculine identity in its integration; Brown's masculine identity is integrated as different, though part of a continuum of masculinity: In both of these masculine identities whiteness is made visible in integration, as a social formation that is accepting and tolerant, masking the hegemony of whiteness as racial superiority. The boyz of Blaxploitation reveal whiteness as a dominating social formation and discourse.

Yet, this revelation of whiteness as domination remains in the standardized form of the escapist narratives of Blaxploitation, remains cathartic in its utopian entertainment form. It is the ensuing debates charted from *Ebony* that the boyz of Blaxploitation raise ethical questions. On the one hand, the black press debates about the men and women of Blaxploitation are presented as concerns of correct or incorrect imagery. On the other, the debates—as debates about community and commitment, the representation of African Americans to the larger American community (quality and the "airing of dirty laundry") and stereotyping—direct one to the ethical dilemma of racial sub-personhood. There are several points to note about this dilemma. First, the debates voice in public discourse a private community concern for representation in a public forum, a concern which informs the cultural production, a generation later, of New Black Cinema. Second, the black press, Blaxploitation, and the debates about representation, the nexus of the three, is an instance of a technology of power, a collective use of Foucaultian technologies which function as maintenance of the African American public. And third, black masculinity, its differences and various forms, becomes the sign of the debate, the vocabulary of public debate and ethical discourse.

The vocabulary of ethical masculinity is most articulate in the representations and *re*-presentations of New Black Cinema. Through the direct engagement with history, media discursivity, and the apparatus of cinema, the masculine ideals and recodings of New Black Cinema supplant the nexus of the press, Blaxploitation, and the debates about Blaxploitation as the technology of power. New Black Cinema uses cinema and entertainment as forums for the projections of critical debate about blackness, cultural citizenship, and American ideals, politics, economics and society, while framing the resolutions to these debates within the unification of the masculine identity. As a technology of power, as a system determining the conduct and behavior of others, New Black Cinema, however, can no longer forcibly frame the questions of blackness, unification and ethics as dilemmas of black masculinity. The sign of the black masculine, the figures of boyz, is no longer so easily defined, nor so singular in its significations.

Arguably, the disintegration of the monolithic boyz as the singular image of black masculinity has broadened the semiotic and discursive fields of representation to offer space for bois and the image of D'Angelo. As a boi D'Angelo's performative ethos certainly engages, indeed "plays" and flirts with boys and boyz. This flirtation, however, is asserted as critical engagement, is critique, is signifyin(g) in its play and reference to boys and boyz. D'Angelo's display of hypermasculinity offers a valuation of blackness, of masculinity and of heterosexuality; yet, through video, performance, and soul music, the valuations are rendered as inadequate and incommensurable to ideals of blackness and masculinity as sites of knowledge and unified subject formations. Race and gender are subjected to a performance of the black masculine self as vulnerability. In the state of vulnerability, indeed a state of nakedness in the video, there is a visualization of the instability of masculinity, the indeterminacy of it and the imperative to manage this instability and indeterminacy through individuation, conduct, and self-realization.

Through the course of this project, I have deliberately *not* done two things: first, I have not tried to perform a ranking or valuing of the propositions of masculinities discussed here. Second, I have not raised the question of gay men, cultural production (for example the work of Marlon Riggs) and an ethics of gender. To note the first, my project has been an excavation; the ordering of figures, Poitier, Brown, Blaxploitation, New Black Cinema, and D'Angelo, are in the order of appearance. All are in exchange with each other and discursively in exchange in the public sphere contemporarily. My efforts have been at elucidating and elaborating the problematics of these figures and the ethical questions that they engender through gender and race.

To note the second, the public figures and the texts that are discussed here are popular figures and texts. I have explicitly chosen them because they are figures and texts which are centrally defining the parameters of questions of ethics and gender, as questions of identification with masculinity and heterosexuality, and within the traditions of the discourse of the person and sub-person. Arguably, I have performed a "queering" or queer reading of the texts and figures, but they themselves engage gender and ethics as identification and tradition. There is a significant amount of work existing on queer subject and gender identification. Indeed, *Boys, Boyz, Bois* is informed by them. Foremost, for my purpose, among this existing body of work is Josè Munoz's (1998) work on disidentification, which better, more appropriately engages the questions of queer performance and cultural production as they relate to ethics, race, ethnicity, and gender. Therefore, I have not, or only obliquely, examined specific queer media production and strategies. Instead, I broadly suggest that notions of gender and race are embedded in categorical thinking and questions and propositions of ethics. By situating these questions in popular public discourse and imagery, I indicate the black masculine identities of discussion are directly in conversation with these categories, questions and propositions. Furthermore, the interrogations of these public figures, identities, and performances present the possibilities and limitations of these categories of race and gender, present the possibilities and limitations as ethical questions and, however problematically they are resolved, present questions of human equality and universality in recognition that there has been a failure in the achievement of equality and universality.

# Notes

## NOTES TO THE INTRODUCTION

1. This construction of race and gender as questions of knowledge and action and the use of knowledge is informed by Paul Ricouer's (1999) discussion of the ethical problematic of memory.

2. Discussion of the temporal and spatial inflections is derived from reading Kant's (1798) *Anthropology from a Pragmatic Point of View,* especially "Part II: Anthropological Characterization," 195–251. This spatial and temporal configuration is also suggested in Kant's (1764) earlier *Observations on the Feeling of the Beautiful and Sublime,* especially in the section, "Of National Characters . . ." (97–116). Also, see Eze (1997), "Introduction," 1–9.

3. The concept of coevalness is taken from Johannes Fabian's (1983) discussions of anthropology's allochronism, or denial of coevalness by device (verses the asynchronicity of anachronism). The denial of coevalness is "a persistent and systematic tendency to place the referent(s) of anthropology in a Time other than the present of the producer of anthropological discourse" (31–32). My use of the term here suggests that there is a similar allochronism in Kant's anthropology and ethical theory in which the phenomenal person, through the denial of personhood, is also denied the temporal relations of being contemporaneous with the ideal person of moral discourse.

4. Mills is not the only philosopher (or novelist, literary theorist, or historian) to categorize notions and practices of race in the duality of status (person/sub-person, superior/inferior, visible/invisible). Note Gordon's (1997b) configuration of person/sub-person (and the result of this duality) as superior and inferior: " . . . [B]lackness functions as an aberration that has to be explained without blaming the system in which it emerges. The system of antiblack racism is lived as a self-justified god in its institutions and its inhabitant's flesh. As a consequence, the bloodhound pursuit of a black body takes on a logic premised upon an identity relation between

fact and value. The system is fact; it is 'what is.' It is absolute. Whatever 'is' is what ought to be and hence ought to have been. The inferior Other becomes a fundamental project for the establishment of the Superior Self, whose superiority is a function of what it *is*" (70).

5. I might add that Mills' project of "relativizing" is akin to both Morrison (1992) and Taylor's (1998), and in turn both of these authors have some influence over my present project. For Morrison, the project is to situate questions of knowledge within the crisis of representation and American literature: "This knowledge holds that traditional, canonical American literature is free of, uninformed, and unshaped by the four-hundred-year-old presence of, first Africans and then African Americans in the United States. It assumes that this presence—which shaped the body politic, the constitution, and the entire history of the culture—has no significant place or consequence in the origin and development of that culture's literature" (4). For Taylor, the relativizing is done through the configuration of the aesthetic (a conceptual model) as an ethnic gaze: "The aesthetic, then, is an ethnic gaze, and a class one at that. It operates in that region where the beliefs of its converts grant it an undeniable reality as a mental object. It is only when that provisional reality is exceeded and the aesthetic is underwritten as a universal category that it becomes identifiable as false consciousness on a staggering scale" (15).

6. Franz Fanon discusses the need to reject philosophical and scientific descriptions of man that cannot address the failure or abuse of these descriptions with regards to race and the "epidermal schema." Fanon proposes to place alongside phylogeny and ontogeny the notion of sociogeny (Fanon 1967, 11). Mills (1998) and Lewis Gordon (1995a and b) favor a sociogenic approach to questions of race and philosophy, specifically to the concept of ontology that provides a description of a universal being at the same time that it posits and constructs a racialized and hierarchized category of man. A sociogenic approach allows for the notion of ontology to be contested through a historized reading of the concepts of being and the category of man.

7. This is not to suggest that only black masculinity is dialogic; indeed, it is more suggestive that any racial or gendered or racially gendered position is inherently dialogic.

8. The other two technologies, to which I do not make specific reference, are implicit in discussions of power and the self: technologies of production and technologies of sign systems. As Foucault notes, each of these four are associated with a certain type of domination, but rarely do they function alone (Foucault 1988, 18).

9. DuBois discusses art throughout his voluminous body of writing. For some of the more pertinent discussions, see DuBois 1903a, 1913, and 1926; for discussions of the "Talented Tenth," see DuBois 1903b.

10. Simultaneity and intersectionality are taken from Valerie Smith's (1998) discussions of black feminism and black feminist theorizing: " . . . I argue that black feminism provides strategies of reading simultaneity. I take as a

given that black feminist inquiry is a site of critique that challenges mono-lithic notions of Americanness, womanhood, blackness, or, for that matter, black womanhood. . . . I use the practice of reading intersectionally to question the implications of ideological and aesthetic liminality" (xv). See Smith 1998; also, on intersectionality see Crenshaw (1989) and Beavers (1997)

11. My account of phenomenology is developed from Merleau-Ponty's theory of the lived body (Merleau-Ponty 1964 and 1962; Madison 1981; and Sobchack 1992), and some explanation of terminology is necessary, as to avoid later confusion. When I speak of phenomenology, I am speaking of three constitutive relations: 1). consciousness and the body; 2). the embod-ied subject (consciousness plus the body) and the world; and 3). the self (the embodied subject) and other people; these three constitutive, interde-pendent relations are what Merleau-Ponty describes as being-in-the-world (Madison 1981, 22). The body is a lived-body, an embodied subject in a relation with itself and the world, in an intrasubjective and intersubjective relation, in a reversible (reflexive) and reciprocal (reflective) relation. The lived-body is a perceptive and expressive and intentional body. Perception is a subjective modality, a bodily situationality from which the world is constituted in meaning (Madison, 40). Expression is an objective modality, a bodily position from which meaning is expressed, from which meaning is signified. The lived-body is the subject's presence and position in the world. The body teaches and informs the self of space and mobility. The body inhabits the world (Madison, 40). As the lived-body is both intrasubjective and intersubjective, every lived-body that is being-in-the-world is simulta-neously in a subjective and objective modality, is both perceptive and expressive. The lived body then denotes existence, an existence that is in a dialectical relationship as both object and subject (Madison, 22). With the intentional body, I work within a Husserlian framework of intentionality, referring to the directedness of consciousness, the conscious subjective awareness of intentions toward an object (be that object real or imaginary or reflexive, *i.e.*, consciousness itself) (Husserl 1965). In this way, all knowledge of the world that arises from an intentional act arises in experi-ence and materializes as a mediated relational experience, as a correlational experience, between consciousness and phenomena. And finally, the notion of the lived-world (*Lebenswelt*) is the world of immediate experience; a human world posited in existence and constituting the intentional fields of action (Bidney 1973, 134). The lived-world of any given society then is a subjective experience (of a perceiving lived-body) and culture that becomes an intersubjective system of meaningful experience (Bidney 134).

12. The notion of critical ontology is taken from Gordon (1995a, 135; and Sec-tion 5, 160–184) and refers to questions of ontology as they are raised by Sartre and Fanon. For Sartre, ontology is existential and attends to the dimensions of being as they are inscribed in the look and the gaze. The Fanonian aspect of critical ontology is found in the methodology of sociogeny (see note 7 above).

13. See, especially in reference to my discussion, the work of Teresa de Lauretis (1984); Patricia Hill Collins (1990); hooks (1992, 1989, and 1984); and Wallace (1990 and 1978).

14. These works include the anthologies edited by Berger, *et. al.* (1995); Brod and Kaufman (1994); and Craig (1992). Other works of influence in this area include: Connell (1995); Craig (1993); Donaldson (1993); Hanke (1992 and 1990); Hearn (1998); and Messner (1997).

15. For discussions of film with specific reference to the representation of male bodies, see, Dyer (1982); Ian Green (1984); Steven Neale (1983); and more recently, Peter Lehman (2001 and 1993)

16. Hanke (1992) makes a similar point about whiteness, locating it in the question of authorship and the men writing about hegemonic masculinity (185–186).

17. For example, the politics of masculinity embedded in the Million Man March (1995), which among other things proposes that black men bond (within a collective masculinity informed by the historical and current images and figures of black men) and return to their families as caretakers and caregivers and provide role models for young black boys. However, the model is steeped in neo-nationalism, religiosity and patriarchal family structures, which exclude alternative masculinities, sexualities and non-normative family structures. The complimentary men's movement (predominately white and middle-class), though informed by the same discourses of nation, religion, and heterosexual reproduction, is not contained by the discourses of deviant criminality or the singularity of exceptionalism, rendering the model of masculinity articulated in the movement as newly liberated from the constraints of masculinity. The return to nation, religion, and family is not from the netherworld of criminality but from overachievement and oppressive over responsibility. Instead of becoming men, the men's movement proposes a model of becoming a better man. See George Yùdice (1995); and Richard Fung (1995) for a more elaborate discussion of the construction of whiteness and responsibility and recuperation in men's movements.

## NOTES TO CHAPTER ONE

1. Also, see Collins (1990) for further discussion of Moynihan's construction of black femininity and the black family as culturally inferior, resulting from the matriarchal family structure and the failure of it as an idealized form of the patriarchal family (75).

2. Indeed, Majors and Billson suggest that their study offers some challenge to the studies and construction of black masculinity since the publication of "The Moynihan Report" (109).

3. As Kelley (1997) notes this is a particular conception of cool pose, one which imposes a gender and trajectory of sexuality (heterosexuality) onto the concept. Thus, cool pose as used by Majors and Billson, for example, elaborates a masculine aesthetic response which precludes discussion and

examination of cool pose as a concept of blackness expressed across gender and sexuality: "By playing down the aesthetics of cool and reducing the cool pose to a response by heterosexual black males to racism, intraracial violence, and poverty, the authors not only reinforces the idea that there is an essential black urban culture created by the oppressive conditions of the ghetto but ignore manifestations of the cool in the public 'performances' of black women, gay black men and the African American middle class" (Kelley, 31–32). Also, see Duneier's (1992) comments about the portrayal of black men in sociology and journalism and the prevalence of the cool pose as the sole frame of reference (20–21).

4. Austin describes the performative as follows: "The term 'performative' is used in a variety of cognate ways and constructions, much as the term 'imperative' is. The name is derived, of course, from 'perform,' as the usual verb with the noun 'action': it indicates that the issuing of the utterance is the performing of the action . . ." (6). See also Butler 1997 and Sedgwick 1993 for greater excavation of Austin and contemporary queer theoretical uses of the performative and performativity.

5. For the theoretical exchanges between Foucault's "statement" and speech act theory, especially Austin and John Searle, see Dreyfus and Rabinow 1982, 44–78.

6. For some of these discussions on race and gender, see Anderson 1983; Christian 1985; Collins 1990; Gates, editor 1988; Gilman 1988 and 1985; hooks 1984; Holmlund 1993; McClintock 1995; and Stoller 1995.

7. Butler does expand her theory and thinking about race and gender performativity in *Bodies That Matter* (1993a) attending to some questions of race and gender performance. Butler's main exploration is through the notion of passing as the simultaneity of racial and sexual difference. However, one might argue that her discussion of passing as gender performance further subordinates questions of performativity to the sole problematic of sexual difference. For a critique of Butler's approach to race, see Fusco 1995, 65–77.

8. It is not my intention to dispense with gender performativity; indeed, it is a useful theory of interpellation and identification. Also, as the maneuver of bracketing that I am about to make in discussion of racial performativity, the bracketing and enclosure of concepts may be necessary for the purpose of clarity and definition. In other words, though I offer criticism here of Butler's failure to take race into account in her early theorizations of performativity, that absence may have been necessary for such an elaboration of gender.

9. Might I add, there is significant overlap and exchange between gender performativity and racial performativity. As is implicit in my discussion here, explicit in other areas of this work, the two discursive formations of gendered and racialized selves are often interconnected and intertwined and determining of each other.

10. The use of Goffman within the concept of racial performativity is deliberately counter to recent elaborations and critiques of race and performance

theory. I deliberately engage Goffman because there is space for slippage and nuance (as in misperception, misperformance, misapprehension, misdirection and distanciation), which are strategic for the reading of racial performance and racial categories. For a critique of Goffman and his use, counter to the use in my project, in theory of racial performativity see Benston (2000), 39.

11. There is a double meaning in Gates use of "double" when discussing signifyin(g). One draws on the idea of double consciousness, and is more implicitly structured in his writing as a valuation of the difference of blackness as a critical structure of feeling (and this is more apparent in *Figures in Black*). The second use of double is within the notion of double-voiced discourse, which he borrows from Mikhail Bakhtin. For Bakhtin, double-voiced discourse is, "All these phenomena (artistic-speech phenomena) . . . share one common trait: discourse in them has a two fold direction—it is directed both toward the referential object of speech, as in ordinary discourse, and toward *another's discourse*, toward *someone else's speech*" [original italics] (105).

12. For other discussions of signifyin(g) in sports (dunking), religion (testifying and sanctifying), and music, see Caponi 1999a; also see Potter (1995) for an extended discussion of signifyin(g) as a musical idiom.

13. Indeed, corporeality and the phenomenal difference of race are already implied in signifyin(g), as an expression of a black person.

14. Also, see Mancini 1980; and Caponi 1999a.

15. Racial performativity is also informed by Baker's (1987 and 1988) notions of cultural performance and black aesthetics. Both are negotiations of form and mastery, as Baker outlines it (Baker 1987, 15; and 1988). Black aesthetics (as mastery of form) and cultural performance (as deformation of mastery) both signify distinctive practices of the self that function as modes of racial critique (1987, 63). Racial performativity deviates from Baker's cultural performance and black aesthetics in that performativity relies more on existential phenomenological methodology as opposed to Baker's Hegelian "spirit work." See Baker 1987, 53–69; and 1988.

16. I would like to point out that by polemical I do not intend a semantic collapse of polemical into the meaning of oppositional as some critics have (see hooks 1992; Caponi 1999b; and to a certain extent, Mills 1998). Blackness and cultural expression of blackness are not, as such, inherently oppositional.

17. I might add that this element of contradiction is apparent in the concept of duality, in the dual (or multiple) social spheres of race, in the dual worlds implied in, for example, racial segregation and racial profiling, and in tropes of duality which provide critical tools for examining these contradictions.

18. Of course, strategic essentialism is in reference to Spivak and deconstructive practices of the critic and representation. See Spivak 1990, 50–58.

19. For other sites of departure see Cripps 1993 and 1977; Lott 1999 and 1991; Smith, 1997a; and Yearwood 2000, 1982a and 1982b.

20. For the relationship between *Birth* and its novel and theatrical predecessor, *The Clansman* (Thomas Dixon), see Franklin (1989, 10–23). For *Birth*'s dependence on and adaptation of literary images and stereotypes of blackness, see Cripps (1977, 1–69); Guerrero (1993, 1–35); and Snead (1994, 37–45). For the innovations of narrative and form in Griffith's cinema see Gunning (1991). For a critique of Griffith's conventional use of film form as a strategy or narrative and narration of whiteness, see Bernardi (1996a, 103–128); and Taylor (1998, Chapter Five; also in Bernardi 1996b, 15–37).

21. By no means was Griffith the first to use these portrayals of black folk (for a pre-history of these images in early Hollywood see Cripps 1977 and Bernardi 1998a). However, Griffith's fluid, dynamic mastery of techniques of editing and lighting and their simultaneous use in the structuration of narrative and story telling melded and established form into classical narrative film convention.

22. For these various histories, see Barnes 1925; Cripps 1977; "Black Writing" in Jones 1966, 161–165; Locke 1925a; "Black Writers Role," (Parts I-III) and "The Black Arts Movement" in Neal 1989, 24–78; Reid 1993; and Yearwood 1982a.

23. Yearwood defines signifying practice as follows: "Signifying practice describes the process we use to make our films, the sum of cinematic languages, aural and visual languages, languages of color, and languages of imagery. It is through various language systems that existing social relations are represented and reproduced" ( 115)

24. Yearwood is very unclear about the question of black film as genre and the relationship of black film to Hollywood. Indeed, Yearwood offers a critique of Cripps (1978), at the same time that he uses generic criteria of convention and narrative to elaborate further the definition of black film as a kind of film. See Yearwood (2000, 87–94).

25. The notion of genricity is taken from Altman's (1999) discussion of the syntactic/semantic approach to genre studies: "We need to recognize that not all genre films relate to their genre in the same way or to the same extent. By simultaneously accepting semantic and syntactic notions of genre we avail ourselves of a possible way to deal critically with differing levels of 'genricity.' In addition, a dual approach permits a far more accurate description of the numerous intergeneric connections typically suppressed by single-minded approaches. It is simply not possible to describe Hollywood cinema accurately without the ability to account for the numerous films that innovate by combining the syntax of one genre with the semantics of another. In fact, it is only when we begin to take up problems of genre history that the full value of the semantic/syntactic approach becomes obvious" (221).

## NOTES TO CHAPTER TWO

1. Discussions of stars, celebrity, stardom, star phenomenon and star vehicles are informed by Britton (1991); Dyer (1979 and 1986); and Marshall

(1997). Specifically for the notion of star vehicle, I rely on Dyer's (1979) definition of star vehicle: "[Star vehicles] were often built around star images. Stories might be expressly written to feature a given star, or books might be bought for production with a star in mind. . . . The vehicle might provide a) a character of the type associated with the star . . . , b) a situation, setting or generic context associated with the star . . . , c) the opportunity for the star to do her/his thing [as in singing or dancing]. . . . As with genres proper, one can discern across a star's vehicle continuities of iconography . . . , visual style . . . , and structure . . ." (70–71).

2.  The primary texts informing my notion of autobiography are as follows: Adell (1994); Andrews (1993a and b and 1991); Butler-Evans (1989); de Man (1984); Gordon (2000); Lejuene (1989); Olney (1993); Paquet (1993); Steptoe (1979 [1991]); and Stone (1993 and 1982).

3.  For Lejuene (1989) and the autobiographical pact, " . . . everything depends, on the one hand, on the link that I establish, through the notion of *author,* between the person and the name; on the other hand, on the fact that I have chosen the perspective of the reader in defining autobiography. [ . . . ] What defines autobiography for the one who is reading is above all a contract of identity that is sealed by the proper name" (19). And for de Man (1984): "Autobiography, thus, is not a genre or a mode, but a figure of reading or of understanding that occurs, to some degree, in all texts. The autobiographical moment happens as an alignment between the two subjects [the subject writing the autobiography and the subject formed in the written autobiography] involved in the process of reading in which they determine each other by mutual reflexive substitution. The structure implies differentiation as well as similarity, since both depend on a substitutive exchange that constitutes the subject. This specular structure is interiorized in a text in which the author declares himself the subject of his own understanding, but this merely makes explicit the wider claim to authorship that takes place whenever a text is stated to be *by* someone and assumed to be understandable to the extent that this is the case. Which amounts to saying that any book with a readable title page is, to some extent autobiographical" (70). De Man continues further, "The specular moment that is part of all understanding reveals the tropological structure that underlies all cognitions, including knowledge of self. The interest of autobiography, then, is not that it reveals reliable self-knowledge—it does not—but that it demonstrates in a striking way the impossibility of closure and of totalization (that is the impossibility of coming into being) of all textual systems made up of tropological substitutions" (71).

4.  The notion of "undecidability," which will occur again in this text, is taken from de Man's comments on autobiography, "[as] not an either/or polarity but that it is undecidable," in the distinction between fiction and autobiography (70). However, the appropriation of "undecidability," here on my part, is sign of indecision about or irresolution to the definitions, parameters, and confines of autobiography as they are brought into question with the practice of African American, as well as immigrant and ethnic, autobiography.

5. Epistemic closure is also identified, by other names, in Harper (1994a). For Harper, closure arrives in the negativity of blackness as a social impossibility: "To a great degree, the difficulty confronted in the constitution of the African American subject is a function of the social interrelation of blacks and whites in the United States. The nature of that interrelation casts black identity necessarily as a problem, an objective never to be realized, hardly to be imagined, so that the black subject exists not so much as the negativity conventionally believed to emblematize it but rather always as potentiality unfulfilled, simultaneous promise and disappointment" (116).

6. All references to *This Life* (Poitier, 1980) are hereafter cited as *TL*.

7. Dyer (1986) presents a useful private/public dichotomous set of oppositions as follows: individual/society; sincere/insincere; country/city; physical/mental; body/brain; naturalness/artifice; sexual intercourse/social intercourse; racial/ethnic; and *viz.* Romanticism and Lacanian psychoanalysis: subconscious/conscious; Id/Ego; Imaginary/Symbolic (11).

8. Dyer (1986) notes of the star biography, which is equally true about the star autobiography, though through the different means of self-presentation: "Star biographies are devoted to the notion of showing us the star as he or she really is. Blurbs, introduction, every page assures us that we are being taken 'behind the scenes,' 'beneath the surface,' 'beyond the image,' there where the truth resides. Or again there is the rhetoric of sincerity or authenticity, . . ." (11).

9. Again, the use of private *versus* public oppositions as a framing discourse of stardom is informed by Dyer (1986). However, in Dyer's discussion of stardom, and especially that of Paul Robeson, the ethnicity-race set is the opposite. For Dyer, race is private and ethnicity is public, a set and order applicable to notions of whiteness which are determined by European ancestry and ethnic stereotyping/marketing in the Hollywood publicity machine. But, where race concerns blackness, I have necessarily reversed this oppositional set. The publicness of blackness as race and the singularity of "black" as a signifier of racial difference (from whiteness) and ethnic erasure (of Africans from the diaspora as culturally and ethnically different from each other) necessitates that there be a re-orientation of ethnic black as private and racial black as public. The distinction, and reversal, becomes important when considering Poitier's upbringing and confluence of immigration and migration and subsequent assimilation into African American black culture.

10. For more on Poitier, and the social problem film, see Cripps (1993), 215–294. For titles, see Appendix II.

11. His father's words were as follows: "' . . . Never beat on a woman. If you ever find that you must beat on a woman then you must leave her. Because if you have to beat on her once, you will have to beat on her again. There is no life for a man who has to reason with his woman through fists. [ . . . ] And another thing you must learn—always take care of your children. Under no circumstance, ever in your life, must you allow yourself to neglect

your children. Take care of your children before you do anything else. That is a law of life'" (*TL*, 230).

12. Harper continues to elaborate the differences: "Insofar as they diverge, these differing demands for simulacral and mimetic realism might be taken to indicate distinct concerns with the soundness of society generally, in the case of the former, and the psychological well-being of blacks specifically, in the case of the latter" (160).

13. And this is most apparent in *In the Heat of the Night*. Specifically there is the scene which parodies this aspect of Poitier's typecasting by having the white, southern sheriff jokingly say, "There'll be none of that for you, huh, Tibbs," as they drive by a field of black workers picking cotton.

14. For a specific discussion of the origins of this debate as the question of the designation of African American *versus* black, a debate encompassing the authentic/inauthentic debate, see Harper (1996), especially 55–77.

15. To note, I say most significant black star of post-WW II, American film. There were other stars before and during Poitier's career (which went roughly from the *No way out* [1950] to *Guess Who's Coming to Dinner* [1967], after which his career as an actor began to wane). These other figures would include the following: pre-dating Poitier were Paul Robeson, Nina Mai McKinney, Lena Horne, Louis Armstrong, Nat King Cole, Ethel Waters, Hattie MacDaniels, and to a lesser extent Juano Hernandez and Canada Lee; contemporary to Poitier were Harry Belafonte, Sammy Davis, Jr., Diahann Caroll and Dorothy Dandridge. Again, however, Poitier is singular because of the longevity of his career; the confinement of that career as an actor, producer, and director (as opposed to the dispersal of his stardom across forms as the ubiquitous "black entertainer"); the marketable success of it and the esteem garnered around him as a black star.

## NOTES TO CHAPTER THREE

1. Furthermore, this places the black body, as the athletic body, into the discourse of the male nude as the universal ideal of beauty. The standard of the male nude, as athletic and strongman, becomes important for the discussion of the economy of the ephebe and the warrior, discussed later. See Dyer 1997; Mandell 1983; Mercer 1994; Solomon-Godeau 1997; and Waugh 1993.

2. And might I note, in reference to Toback's description of Brown and Sedgwick's "orbit of desire" in homosociality, that Toback's description of Brown engages the spectatorial desire as homosocial desire, as homoeroticism, in the appreciation of Brown's physique as redemption of the masculine self.

3. As the American democratic ethos, the relationship between the black buddy and white buddy becomes " . . . the spectacle of middle-class life providing the representation of American as embodiment of its own democratic ideals. While the alignment of black females with the representational space most often reserved for white women initiates the democratic ethos, it is the relationship between black and white men that is the film's pivotal site for democratic wholeness" (Wiegman 1991, 320–321).

4. Here I am not only referring to King's "cultural economy of the human body," but also to Robyn Wiegman's "economics of visibility" and her discussion of the visuality of the black body in nineteenth and twentieth century scientific texts. See King (1991) and Wiegman (1995).

5. For more elaborate and detailed discussions of the overlapping trends of social, economic, and aesthetic thought and practice informing this moment of exchange between Hollywood and cultural blackness, see Cripps 1993 and Guerrero 1993, especially; but also see Benston 2000; Bogle 1988, 1980, and 1973; Caponi 1999a; Dyson 1997, 1994, and 1993; Elam 2001a and b; George 1994; Guillory and Green 1998; Johnson 1965 and 1959; Lott 1991; Maynard 1974; Rocchio 2000; Shohat and Stam 1994; Simon 1998; Smith 1997a and b; Watkins 1998; and Yearwood 2000 and 1982a and b.

6. Doherty traces the initial shift in the industry meaning of exploitation (from a descriptive term for marketing any film to a descriptive of a kind of film) to the '50s: " . . . [T]he '50's exploitation picture favored the bizarre, the licentious, and the sensational—and, following the Hollywood mainstream, depicted same with escalating daring and explicitness. In delving unashamedly into often disreputable content and promoting it in an always disreputable manner, the 'exploitation' label acquired a pejorative distinction its exemplars usually lived up to" (8). For a detailed look at exploitation which examines the form before the teenpic, '50s and Doherty's historical time frame, see Schaefer 1999.

7. This has not always been the case with *Ebony,* or the black press broadly. As Charlene Regester (1994) notes of the function of the black press in the black public sphere until the early 1950s: "Particularly during the early years, African Americans frequently found themselves invisible, excluded, alienated, isolated and ignored by the white press. . . . [T]he African American press was instrumental in articulating the views and concerns of the African American community regarding their portrayals on the motion picture screen. The black press was outspoken in denouncing demeaning portrayals in motions pictures, outspoken in condemning African Americans who participated in perpetuating these objectionable images; and outspoken in expressing opposition to the treatment that African Americans received in the motion picture industry" (503). One reason for the shift in the critical stance of *Ebony* (I would not venture to say this about black press across the board) might be that *Ebony*'s critique of black public figures has become more implicit (journalistically, more objective) through its increasing coverage of black America's Talented Tenth. See also Bogle's (1980) comments on *Ebony*'s critique of Eartha Kitt in the 1950s (124–128).

## NOTES TO CHAPTER FOUR

1. The manifesto references the filmmakers Spike Lee, the Hudlin brothers, and Robert Townsend; the playwright George Wolfe; the comedian Eddie

Murphy; the ska/funk/rock/raggae band Fishbone; and an assortment of east coast, neo-nationalist rap bands and artists.

2. There are several reasons for limiting the discussion of New Black Cinema to black masculinity. First, the three films of analysis (*School Daze, House Party, Boyz in the Hood*) are masculinist narratives of coming of age and passing, narratives which foreground the construction and maintenance of masculinity. Second, the initial outpouring product in the mid-80s to early 90s was mostly by men and arguably made for and marketed to young, urban male audiences. Third, the absence of the discussion of femininity and black women is only absent as direct discussion: as the analyses demonstrate, masculinity and feminity are linked, interconnected and wholly dependent upon one another.

3. These films include *Do the Right Thing, House Party, Def by Temptation, Juice, A Rage in Harlem, New Jack City, Five Heartbeats, Boyz N the Hood, Jungle Fever, Mo' Better Blues, Chameleon Street, School Daze, Straight Outta Brooklyn, Harlem Nights.*

4. For example, see the three images, and their differences, among Nola Darling's suitors in Spike Lee's *She's Gotta Have It.*

5. Spike Lee (1988), 179.

6. Dyer defines the utopian sensibilities as follows: energy, the capacity to act vigorously; human power, activity, potential (e.g. dance); abundance, the conquest of scarcity; having enough to spare without sense of poverty of other; enjoyment of sensuous material reality (e.g., spectacle); intensity, experiencing of emotion directly, fully, unambiguously, "authentically' without holding back (e.g., "incandescent" star performers); transparence, a quality of relationships—between represented characters, between performer and audience (e.g., sincere stars; love and romance); and community, togetherness, sense of belonging, network of phatic relationships (e.g., sing-along chorus numbers). See Dyer 1981.

7. Here I am referring to Mulvey's "Visual Pleasure and Narrative Cinema." However, I will not attempt to engage in questions of spectatorship. At this point, I am interested in Lee's structuring of the male gaze. See Mulvey (1989).

8. Reginald Hudlin interviewed in Glicksman (1990).

9. Warrington Hudlin argues that this scene is anti-rape (*versus* anti-gay): "The point is, the guy is in danger of being raped. We're not taking a position on homosexuality, we're taking a position on sex against someone's will." However, the confinement of the anti-rape discourse to a homosocial space of the prison cell directs the viewer not only to the potential of rape but also to rape as forced homosexuality; see Glicksman (1990)

10. See Lisa Kennedy's (1990) reading of Bilial.

11. John Singleton interviewed in Thomas Doherty and Jaquie Jones (1991).

12. Here I am using Judith Mayne's notion of the limit and horizon. See Mayne (1991).

13. For more discussion of this see Guerrero 1998.

14. Films like *Panther* (Mario Van Peebles 1995); *Dead Presidents* (The Hughes Brothers 1995); *Clockers* (Spike Lee 1995); and *Devil in a Blue Dress* (Carl Franklin 1995), for example.

15. This is most apparent in the increased and increasing number of black male stars and celebrities: Denzel Washington, Will Smith, Eddie Murphy, Ice-T, Ice Cube, Samuel Jackson, Laurence Fishbourne, Roger Guenevere Smith, Savion Glover, Cedric the Entertainer, Bernie Mac, Steve Harvey, Chris Rock, Chris Tucker, Jamie Foxx, to name a few. And also the expansion of the role of the thug or the gangsta to that of the anti-hero in American film, for example Ice Cube's character in *Ghost of Mars* (John Carpenter 2001) or *XXX: State of the Union* (Lee Tamahori 2005) and Snoop Doggy Dogg's character in *Bones* (Ernest Dickerson 2001).

16. Indeed, one can examine John Singleton's return to the hood film, a genre and black male narrative which he, arguably, formalized, and the closure of that genre and narrative in *Baby Boy* (2001). In this film Singleton re-writes the ambiguous and abject figure of the gangsta, Doughboy (Ice Cube) from *Boyz N the Hood* (1991), as threat, menace and impossibility in the imagined black community, through the annihilation of the gangsta character Rodney (Snoop Dogg) in the protection of family and class and economic mobility. The archetypal gangsta character, which functioned as the consciousness of the black community in so many hood films, is no longer viable and, instead, replaced by the conscientious, jobless, yet upwardly mobile, "baby boy" (Jody as portrayed by Tyrese Gibson), a fig-ure of mockery and revision.

## NOTES TO CHAPTER FIVE

1. Indeed, it may be argued that D'Angelo has not reached star status as a musician and performer. For the distinction in music between star and auteur, see Roy Shuker, *Understanding Popular Music (Second Edition)* (London and New York: Routledge 2001), 115–137.

2. This image change is also part of the spiritual quest/journey expressed in D'Angelo's flirtation with *voudou:* "The idea came to me from a whole bunch of different sources, but the main reason that ties everything together is that I had so many visions of ceremonies or things that had to do with being in a trance, or being possessed by a spirit, and it all being done with or through music, son, and dance. I wanted to really make a statement about how powerful music is, that music is a spirit within itself, and that music can be a bridge to a spiritual realm." See Quest-love, np.

3. The image is present in images like Brad Pitt in a sequence cocktail dress on the cover of *Vanity Fair* promoting the film *Fight Club* to increased male nudity in film to the bare-chested, head wrapped hip-hop rappers and soul singers like the late Tupac, Usher, DMX, and D'Angelo.

4. Andrew Ross notes that the spectrum of the black masculine is capped at both poles by the figures of the gangsta and the diva, who, on the margins of black masculinity, are the limits of black masculinity. What is disturbing about Ross's configuration of black masculinities is the formations of them in a romanticization of a moment of expressive black culture and the valorization of exceptional singular masculinities, which, as such, are already contained and disciplined in their publicness, commercialization, and in their status as icons.

The romance of gangsta rap and black drag queens can be located in Ross's discussion of ghetto realism and drag queen realness, which he attributes to the style and aesthetics of gangstas and drag queens. Yet, these received aesthetics of the real are built upon the maintenance of an ever unchanging changing of the lives of mostly urban, inner city young black men. Telling in Ross's critique is his exposition of "frontin,'" an aesthetic and stylistic appropriation of the community voice of urban black men, and "representin,'" a more authentic community voicing, story-telling, and, to a certain extent, activism (162). The status of the celebrity rappers as representatives requires maintenance of the community of listeners. The community of listeners, however, as it is maintained, must reproduce a disenfranchised population of black men. (Granted there are social and political mechanisms at work, for example, the condition of many inner city areas being police states, which contribute to the social conditions of young black men; however, in Ross and gangsta rappers' jargon of authenticity, the very real mechanisms at work are disarticulated as the conditions and re-articulated as justification for the violence imposed and sanctioned from within and without these communities.) To maintain the iconicity of gangsta masculinity, rappers must continue a ghettoization, a nihilistic self-representation of violence and valor, fixing a self-imploding masculinity in the very discourses of experience, authenticity and community self-determination which produce them.

Moreover, Ross's discussion of drag queens and RuPaul, through his elision of the differences among drag queens and the popular appropriation of drag, serves to ignore the deracination of drag from sexuality. First, Ross unproblematically equates RuPaul to the community of drag queens in *Paris is burning* (160). This equation ignores the evolution of RuPaul as an art school trained performer, making a living off drag performances versus the denizens of Harlem's drag balls who have appropriated drag as a lifestyle, often living off drag not as a performer (at least not within the same performance arena as RuPaul) and public personae, but as sexual workers catering to the appetites of sexual exoticism. One could also argue that RuPaul and the Harlem voguers are of two different schools of drag, the downtown Wigstock and the uptown ball, respectively. These two schools articulate a different strategy in the use and performance of drag, one of parody, almost slapstick and the other a technique of the self. Indeed, as Ross notes, there may be an elsewhere proposed and a utopian impulse in the performance of gender and glamour in the Harlem balls, but this is the very utopian impulse which is lost in the figure of RuPaul, who, as a popular image, can only articulate a discourse of asexual love, a sort of new age/feel good discourse of the self which negates the technique of self and body which the Harlem ball drag proposes (165).

What is further lost in the focus on RuPaul as emblematic of drag masculinity is the violent dynamic of the co-existent masculinities. Ross notes that both gangstas and drag queens re-produce similar structures of community and family, both emerging from poverty and the ghetto and structured in loyalty, both reforming community and family in the absence of family and exclusion of family. It is sexuality and sexual practice, however, which leaves these two communities in violent opposition to each other. The co-existence of these two figures in popular culture is the a process of de-politicization, de-sexualization, and dis-identification, which, on the one hand, is recuperated and constantly re-articulated as authenticity in the gangsta rapper's mining of the inner city in order to participate in the public regime of black masculinity and, on the other hand, is celebrated through the language of love and tolerance in the image of the asexual RuPaul.

It is the asexualization process (a negation of masculine difference rendering all difference as the same) which allows for drag non-threateningly and uncritically to be inserted into the pantheon of black masculinity. This asexualization is also indicative of current debates and theories of masculinity and new masculinities: By instituting a catalogue or taxonomy of difference within the trope of ideal or racialized masculinity, activists and cultural theorists often fail to disrupt the structure of masculinity, and instead alternative, non-masculine, or critical masculinities are recuperated in a *telos* in which heterosexual masculinity is reconstructed and reaffirmed. See Andrew Ross, "The Gangsta and the Diva," in Thelma Golden, editor, *Black Male: Representation of Masculinity in Contemporary America* (New York: Whitney Museum of American Art, 1994), 159–166.

6. For the liner notes, see Saul Williams, "Like the rain to the dirt from vine to the wine from the alpha of creation" (London and New York: Virgin Records, 1999) liner notes to *Voodoo*.

7. There has been some discussion of the song and its video visualization as a song about oral sex: The question "How does it feel," then, is about fellatio. However, I do not think that the question is that graphically directed, in that it is not directed to a sexual act, but more to the incommensurability of sexuality and sexual difference. The immediate points of reference for my reading would be D'Angelo's ethos and discursive paratextuality (which by no means excludes oral sex as a pleasure or possibility) and their emphases on a movement of pleasure to a point of excess beyond the body and in the spirit; and the second point of reference would be Warhol's *Blow Job* (Andy Warhol 1963). Juxtaposing *Blow Job* and "How does it feel" reveals the two pieces to have two different relationships to masculinity: In *Blow Job,* the inscription of masculine pleasure in

the realist mode of the long take affirms masculinity as knowable by the specificity of the act of fellatio and the documentation of that act; in "How does it feel," the act, if there at all, is irrelevant because there is the undermining of masculinity as something that is knowable without the confirmation of an other. Also see D'Angelo's comments in Hampton 2000 and Questlove 1999.

8. Mercer's use of *ambivalence* is informed by Homi Bhabha's concept of the repetition of the fixity in colonial discourse and colonial fantasy, a fixity which limits the representation, in this case, of blackness to the reproductions of fantasies of black sexuality. For Bhabha, ambivalence is central to understanding the stereotype: "For it is the force of ambivalence that gives the colonial stereotype its currency: ensures its repeatability in changing historical and discursive conjunctures; informs its strategies of individuation and marginalisation; produces that effect of probabilistic truth and predictability which, for the stereotype, must always be in *excess* of what can be empirically proved or logically construed." See Homi Bhabha, "The other Question: The Stereotype and Colonial Discourse," *Screen* 24 (1983): 18–36.

9. McClintock's reading and re-conceptualization fetishism is in an effort to understand femininity and the impossibility of it in Freudian and Lacanian psychoanalysis and in an effort to foreground the sedimentations of race and racial categories embedded in the history and uses of the concept. See also William Pietz, "The Problem of the Fetish, I," *Res* 9 (Spring 1985): 5–17.

10. The notion of "ethical incompleteness" is taken from the work of Ian Hunter. Ethical incompleteness refers to the exchange between a reader/critic and the text, an exchange in which the task of the reader becomes one of inscribing indeterminancy in relation to the text that guarantees the reader's ethical incompleteness at the same time that the reader is inscribed as an exemplary reader. In reference to D'Angelo and the music video for "Untitled," D'Angelo, arguably, performs a reading of race and masculinity through performance in the video. See Ian Hunter, *Culture and Government* (London and New York: Routledge, 1988).

# Bibliography

Adell, Sandra. 1994. *Double Consciousness/Double Bind: Theoretical Issues in Twentieth-Century Black Literature*. Chicago and Urbana: University of Illinois Press.

Adorno, Theodor W. 1973. *The Jargon of Authenticity*. A translation of *Jargon der Eigentlichkeit: Aur deutschen Ideologie* (1964). Translated by Knut Tarnowski and Frederic Will. Evanston: Northwestern University Press.

Allen, Ernest, Jr. 1997. "On the Reading of Riddles: Rethinking DuBoisian 'Double Consciousness.'" In *Existence in Black,* edited by Lewis Gordon, 49–68. London and New York: Routledge.

Altman, Rick. 1999. *Film/Genre*. London: British Film Institute.

Anderson, Benedict. 1983. *Imagined Communities*. London and New York: Verso.

Andrews, William. 1993a."Introduction." In *African-American Autobiography: A Collection of Critical Essays,* edited by William L. Andrews, 1–8. Englewood, New Jersey: Prentice Hall.

———, ed. . 1993b. *African-American Autobiography: A Collection of Critical Essays*. Englewood, New Jersey: Prentice Hall.

———. 1991. "African-American Autobiography Criticism: Retrospect and Prospect." In *American Autobiography,* edited by Paul John Eakin, 195–215. Madison: University of Wisconsin Press.

Appiah, Kwame Anthony. 1993. "'No Bad Nigger': Blacks as the ethical principle in movies." In *Media Spectacles,* edited by Marjorie Barber, Jann Matlock and Rebecca L. Walkowitz, 77–90. London and New York: Routledge.

———. 1992. *In My Father's House*. New York and Oxford: Oxford University Press.

Archer-Straw, Petrine. 2000. *Negrophilia: Avant-Garde Paris and Black Culture in the 1920's*. London: Thames and Hudson.

Austin, J.L. 1962. *How to do things with words: The William James Lectures delivered at Harvard University in 1955*. Edited by J.O. Urmson and Marina Sbisà. Cambridge, MA: Harvard University Press.

Balshaw, Maria. 2000. *Looking for Harlem: Urban Aesthetics in African-American Literature*. London and Sterling, Virginia: Pluto Press.

Baker, Houston, Jr. 1993. *Black Studies, Rap and the Academy.* Chicago and London: University of Chicago Press.

———. 1988. *Afro-American Poetics: Revisions of Harlem and the Black Aesthetic.* London and Madison: University of Wisconsin Press.

———. 1987. *Modernism and the Harlem Renaissance.* Chicago and London: University of Chicago Press.

Bakhtin, Mikhail. 1984. "Double-Voiced Discourse in Dostoevsky." Translated by C. Emerson. Excerpted from *Problems of Dostoevsky's Poetics* (Minneapolis: University of Minnesota Press). In *The Bakhtin Reader,* edited by Pam Morris, 102–112. New York: Edward Arnold.

Bambara, Toni Cade. 1991. "Programming with *School Daze.*" In *Five by Five: The Films of Spike Lee,* edited by Shirley L. Poole, 47–55. New York: Stewart, Tabori & Chang, Inc.

Barnes, Albert. 1925. "Negro Art and America." In *The New Negro,* edited by Locke, 19–25. New York: Macmillan Publishing.

Barton, Rebecca Chalmers. 1948. *Witnesses for Freedom: Negro Americans in Autobiography.* London and New York: Harper & Brothers Publishers.

Batchen, Geoffrey. 1996. *Burning with Desire: The Conception of Photography.* Cambridge, Massachusetts: MIT Press.

Bayars, Jackie. 1991. *All That Hollywood Allows: Re-Reading Gender in the 1950's Melodrama.* Chapel Hill: University of North Carolina Press.

Baudrillard, Jean. 1983. *Simulations.* Translated from French by Paul Foss, Paul Patton, and Phillip Beitchman. New York: Semiotext(e), Inc.

Beavers, Herman. 1997. "'Cool Pose': Intersectionality, Masculinity and Quiescence in the Comedy and Films of Richard Pryor and Eddie Murphy." In *Race and the Subject of Masculinities,* edited by Harry Stecopolus and Michael Ubel, 253–285. Durham, NC: Duke University Press.

Benston, Kimberly. 2000. *Performing Blackness: Enactments of African-American Modernism.* London and New York: Routledge.

Bercovitch, Sacvan. 1982. "The Ritual of American Autobiography: Edwards, Franklin, Thoreau." *Revue française d'ètudes amèricaines,* 14: 139–150.

Berger, Maurice, Brian Wallis, and Simon Watson, eds. 1995. *Constructing Masculinity.* London and New York: Routledge.

Bernardi, Daniel, ed. 2001. *Classic Hollywood, Classic Whiteness.* Minneapolis: University of Minnesota Press.

———. 1996a. "The Voice of Whiteness." In *The Birth of Whiteness,* edited by Bernardi, 103–128. London and New York: Routledge.

———, ed. 1996b. *The Birth of Whiteness: Race and the Emergence of US Cinema.* London and New York: Routledge.

Bhabha, Homi. 1983. "The Other Question: The Stereotype and Colonial Discourse." *Screen* 24: 6, 18–36.

Bidney, Marcus. 1973. " Phenomenological Method and the Anthropological Science of the Cultural Life-World." In *Phenomenology and the Social Sciences, Volume 1,* edited by Maurice Nathanson. Evanston: Northwestern University Press.

Bingham, Dennis. 1994. *Acting Male: Masculinities in the Films of James Stewart, Jack Nicholson, and Clint Eastwood.* London and New York: Routledge.

Blount, Marcellus and George P. Cunningham, eds. 1996. *Representing Black Men.* London and New York: Routledge.

Boelhower, William. 1991. "The Making of Ethnic Autobiography in the United States." In *American Autobiography: Retrospect and Prospect,* edited by Paul John Eakin, 123–141. London and Madison: The University of Wisconsin Press.

Bogle, Donald. 1988. *Blacks in American Film and Television: An Encyclopedia.* London and New York: Garland Publishing, Inc.

———. 1980. *Brown Sugar: Eighty Years of American's Black Female Superstars.* New York: Da Capo Press. Inc.

———. 1973. *Toms, Coons, Mulattoes, Mammies & Bucks: An Interpretive History of Blacks in American Films.* New York: Continuum, reprinted in 1994.

Bourdieu, Pierre. 1993. *The Field of Cultural Production: Essays on Art and Literature.* Edited and Introduced by Randall Johnson. New York: Columbia University Press.

———. 1990. *The Logic of Practice.* Translated from *Le sense pratique* (1980) by Richard Nice. Stanford, CA: Stanford University Press.

Bourne, Stephen. 1998. *Black in the British Frame.* London and Washington: Cassell.

Boyd, Todd. 1997. *Am I Black Enough for You?* Bloomington: Indiana University Press.

———. 1994. "Check yo self, before you wreck yo self." *Public Culture,* 7:1 (Fall), 289–312.

———. 1989. "Response to Trey Ellis's 'The New Black Aesthetic.'" *Callaloo* 12 (1): 244–246.

Britton, Andrew. 1991. "Stars and Genre." In *Stardom: Industry of Desire,* edited by Christine Gledhill, 198–206. London and New York: Routledge.

Brod, Harry and Michael Kaufaman, editors. 1994. *Theorizing Masculinities.* London: Sage Publications.

Brodesser, Claude. 2000. "NAACP seeks the birth of a diverse Hollywood." *Variety* (February 7, 2000), n. pag. Online. Findarticles.com. 8/12/00.

Brown, Claudine K. 1994. "Mug Shot: Suspicious Person." In *Picturing Us,* edited by Deborah Willis, 137–145. New York: The New Press.

Buell, Lawrence. 1991. "Autobiography in the American Renaissance." In *American Autobiography: Retrospect and Prospect,* 47–69. Madison, Wisconsin: The University of Wisconsin Press.

———. 1973. *Literary Transcendentalism: Style and Vision in American Renaissance.* Ithaca and London: Cornell University Press.

Butler, Jeremy, editor. 1991. *Star Text: Image and Performance in Film and Television.* Detroit: Wayne State University Press.

Butler, Judith. 1997. *Excitable Speech: A politics of the performative.* London and New York: Routledge.

———. 1993a. *Bodies That Matter: On the Discursive Limits of "Sex."* London and New York: Routledge.

———. 1993b. "Critically Queer." *GLQ,* 1(1): 17–32.

———. 1990. *Gender Trouble: Feminism and the Subversion of Identity.* London and New York: Routledge.

Butler-Evans, Elliot. 1989. *Race, Gender and Desire: Narrative Strategies in Fiction of Toni Cade Bambara, Toni Morrison, and Alice Walker.* Philadelphia: Temple University Press.

Butters, Gerald, Jr. 2002. *Black Manhood on the Silent Screen.* Lawrence, Kansas: University Press.

Campbell, Colin. 1987. *The Romantic Ethic and the Spirit of Modern Consumerism.* Oxford, UK and Cambridge, USA: Blackwell.

Caponi, Gina Dagel. 1999a. "Introduction: A Case for an African- American Aesthetic." In *Signifyin(g), Sanctifyin,' and Slam Dunking,* edited by Caponi, 1–31. Amherst: University of Massachusetts Press.

———, ed. 1999b. *Signifyin(g), Sanctifyin,' and Slam Dunking.* Amherst: University of Massachusetts Press.

Carby, Hazel. 1998. *Race Men.* Cambridge, MA and London: Harvard University Press.

Christian, Barbara. 1985. *Black Feminist Criticism: Perspectives on Black Women.* New York: Pergamon Press.

Cohan, Steven, 1997. *Masked: Masculinity and the Movies in the Fifties.* Bloomington: Indiana University Press.

Cole, Patrick. 1992. "Cinema Revolution." *Emerge* (January): 36–40.

Coleman, Daniel. 1995. "Hustling Status, Scamming Manhood: Race, Performance, and Masculinity in Austin Clarke's Fiction." *Masculinities,* 3:1 (Spring): 74–88.

Collins, Patricia Hill. 1990. *Black Feminist Thought: Knowledge, Consciousness, and the Politics of Empowerment.* Boston and London: Unwin Hyman.

Connell, R.W. 1995. *Masculinities.* Berkeley and Los Angeles: University of California Press.

Cook, Pam. 1993. "Introduction: Border Crossings: Women and Film in Prospect." In *Women and Film: A Sight and Sound Reader.* Edited by Pam cook and Phillip Dodd. Philadelphia: Temple University Press, ix-xxiii.

Craig, Steve.1993. "Selling Masculinities, Selling Femininities: Multiple Genders and the Economics of Television." *The Mid-Atlantic Almanac,* Volume 2: 15–27.

———, editor. 1992. *Men, Masculinity, and the Media.* London: Sage Publications.

Crenshaw, Kimberlé W. 1989. "Demarginalizing the Intersection of Race and Sex." *The University of Chicago Legal Forum,* 139–67.

Cripps, Thomas. 1993. *Making Movies Black: The Hollywood Message Movies from World War II to the Civil Rights Era.* New York: Oxford University Press.

———. 1978. *Black Film as Genre.* Bloomington: Indiana University Press.

———. 1977. *Slow Fade to Black.* New York: Oxford University Press.

D'Angelo. 1999. *Voodoo.* London and New York: Virgin Records.

D'Angelo and Raul Saadiq. 1999. "Untitled (How does it feel)." On *Voodoo,* by D'Angelo. New York: Universal-Polygram International Publishing.

Davis, Melody. 1991. *The Male in Contemporary Photography.* Philadelphia: Temple University Press.

Dates, Jannette and William Barlow, Editors. 1991. *Split Images: African-Americans in the Mass Media*. Washington, D. C.: Howard University.

Davey, Nicholas. 1999. "The Hermeneutics of Seeing." In *Interpreting Visual Culture*, edited by Ian Heywood and Barry Sandywell, 3–29. London and New York: Routledge.

De Lauretis, Teresa. 1987. *Technologies of Gender*. Bloomington: Indiana University Press.

———. 1984. *Alice Doesn't: Feminism, Semiotics, Cinema*. Bloomington: Indiana University Press.

De Man, Paul. 1984. *The Rhetoric of Romanticism*. New York: Columbia University Press.

Dent, Gina, editor. 1992. *Black Popular Culture*. Seattle: Bay Press.

Denzin, Norman K. 2002. *Reading Race: Hollywood and the Cinema of Racial Violence*. London: Sage Publications.

Dews, Peter. 1987. *Logics of Disintegration: Post-Structuralist Thought and the Claims of Critical Theory*. London and New York: Verso.

Diawara, Manthia. 1998. *In Search of Africa*. Cambridge, Massachusetts and London: Harvard University Press.

———. 1996. "Absent One." In *Representing Black Men*, edited by Blount and Cunningham, 205–225. London and New York: Routledge.

———. 1993a. "Black American Cinema: The New Realism." In *Black American Cinema*, edited by Diawara, 3–25. London and New York: Routledge

———, ed. 1993b. *Black American Cinema*. London: Routledge.

Dixon, Bobby R. 1997. "Toting Technology." In *Existence in Black*, edited by Gordon, 137–148. London and New York: Routledge.

Doherty, Thomas. 1988. *Teenager and Teen Pics: The Juvenilization of American Movies in the 1950's*. Winchester, MA: Unwin Hyman, Inc.

Doherty, Thomas and Jacquie Jones. 1991 "Two Takes on *Boyz N the Hood*." *Cineaste*, 18 (4): 16–19.

Donaldson, Mike. 1993. "What is hegemonic masculinity?" *Theory and Society*, 22: 643–657.

Doy, Gen. 2000. *Black Visual Culture: Modernity and Postmodernity*. London and New York: I.B.Tauris.

DuBois, W.E.B. 1926. "Criteria of Negro Art." Reprinted in *DuBois Writings*, Library of America, Volume 34. Edited by Nathan Huggins, 993–1002. New York: Penguin Books USA.

———. 1920. *Darkwater: Voices from behind the Veil*. Reprinted in *DuBois Writings*, The Library of America, Volume 34 (1986). Edited by Nathan Huggins, 923–938. New York: Penguin Books USA.

———. 1913. "The Negro in Literature and Art." Reprinted in *DuBois Writings*, Library of America, Volume 34. Edited by Nathan Huggins, 862–867. New York: Penguin Books USA.

———. 1903a. *The Souls of Black Folks*. Reprinted in *DuBois Writings*, The Library of America, Volume 34 (1986). Edited by Nathan Huggins, 357–547. New York: Penguin Books USA.

———. 1903b. "The Talented Tenth." Reprinted in *DuBois Writings*, Library of America, Volume 34. Edited by Nathan Huggins, 842–861. New York: Penguin Books USA.

———. 1897. "The Conservation of Races." Reprinted in *DuBois Writings*, The Library of America, Volume 34 (1986). Edited by Nathan Huggins, 815–826. New York: Penguin Books USA.

Dreyfus, Hubert L. and Paul Rabinow. 1982. *Michel Foucault: Beyond Structuralism and Hermeneutics*. Chicago: University of Chicago Press.

Duneier, Mitchell. 1992. *Slim's Table: Race, Respectability, and Masculinity*. Chicago and London: the University of Chicago Press.

Dyer, Richard. 1997. *White*. London and New York: Routledge.

———. 1986. *Heavenly Bodies: Film Stars and Society*. London: The MacMillan Press Ltd.

———. 1982. "Don't Look Now: The Male Pin-Up." *Screen*, Volume 23 (3–4): 61–73.

———. 1981. "Entertainment and Utopia." In *Genre: The Musical*, edited by Rick Altman, 175–189. London: Routledge & Kegan Paul.

———. 1979. *Stars*. London: British Film Institute.

Dyson, Michael. 1997. *Race Rules: Navigating the Color Line*. New York: Vintage Books.

———. 1994. *Between God and Gangsta Rap: Bearing Witness to Black Culture*. New York and Oxford: Oxford University Press.

———. 1993. *Reflecting Black: African-American Cultural Criticism*. London and Minneapolis: University of Minnesota Press.

Eakin, Paul John, editor. 1991. *American Autobiography: Retrospect and Prospect*. Madison, Wisconsin: The University of Wisconsin Press.

Early, Gerald. 1993a. "Introduction." In *Lure and Loathing*, edited by Gerald Early, xi-xxiv. New York: Penguin Books.

———, editor. 1993b. *Lure and Loathing*. New York: Penguin Books.

Elam, Harry J., Jr. 2001a. "The device of race: An introduction." In *African American Performance and Theater History*, edited by Harry J. Elam, Jr. and David Krasner, 3–16, New York and Oxford: Oxford University Press.

———. 2001b. "The black performer and the performance of blackness." In *African American Performance and Theater History*, edited by Harry J. Elam, Jr. and David Krasner, 288–305. New York and Oxford: Oxford University Press.

Elam, Harry J., Jr. and David Drasner, editors. 2001. *African American Performance and Theater History*. New York and Oxford: Oxford University Press.

Ellis, John. 1982. *Visible Fictions*. London: Routledge.

Ellis, Trey. 1989a. "The New Black Aesthetic." *Callaloo*, 12 (1): 233–243.

———. 1989b. "Responses to NBA Critiques." *Callaloo*, 12 (1): 250–251

Ellison, Ralph. 1953. *Shadow and Act*. New York: Random House.

Everett, Wendy, editor. 2000. *The Seeing Century: Film, Vision, and Identity*. Amsterdam and Atlanta: Radopi.

Eze, Emmanuel Chukwudi, editor. 1997. *Race and the Enlightenment: A Reader*. Cambridge, MA and Oxford: Blackwell Publishers.

Fabian, Johannes. 1983. *Time and the Other: How Anthropology Makes Its Object*. New York: Columbia University Press.

Fanon, Franz. 1967. *Black Skins, White Masks*. New York: Grove Wiedenfeld.

Ferguson, Russell, Martha Gever, Trinh T. Minh-ha, and Cornel West, editors. 1990. *Out There: Marginalization and Contemporary Cultures*. Cambridge, MA and London, England: MIT Press.

"Football Heroes Invade Hollywood." *Ebony* 24 (October 1969): 195–202.

Foucault, Michel. 1988. *Technologies of the Self: A Seminar with Michel Foucault*. Eds. Luther H. Martin, *et al*. Amherst: University of Massachusetts Press.

———. 1972. *The Archeology of Knowledge and the Discourse on Language*. Translated by A.M. Sheridan Smith and Rupert Sawyer. New York: Pantheon Books, 1972.

Franklin, John Hope. 1989. *Race and History: Selected Essays 1938–1988*. Baton Rouge: Louisiana State University Press.

Freeland, Cynthia and Thomas E. Wartenberg, editors. 1995. *Philosophy and Film*. London and New York: Routledge.

Friedman, Lester, Editor. 1991. *Unspeakable Images*. Urbana and Chicago: University of Chicago Press.

Fung, Richard. 1995. "Burdens of Representation, Burdens of Responsibility." In *Constructing Masculinity*, edited by Maurice Berger, *et. al.*, 291–298.

Fusco, Coco. 1995. *English is broken here: Notes on Cultural Fusion*. New York: New Press.

Gamson, Joshua. 1994. *Claims to Fame: Celebrity in Contemporary Culture*. Berkeley and Los Angeles: University of California Press.

Garber, Marjorie, Jann Matlock, and Rebecca Walkowitz, eds. 1993. *Media Spectacles*. London and New York: Routledge.

Gardiner, Michael. 1999. "Bakhtin and the Metaphorics of Perception." In *Interpreting Visual Culture*, edited by Ian Heywood and Barry Sandywell, 58–73. London and New York: Routledge.

Garofalo, Reebee. 1991. "Crossing Over: 1939–1989." In *Split Images: African Americans in the Mass Media*, edited by Jannette Dates and William Barlow, 57–121. Washington, D.C.: Howard University Press.

Gates, Henry Louis, Jr., editor. "Black Man's Burden." In *Black Popular Culture*, edited by Dent, 75–83. Seattle: Seattle Bay Press.

———. 1990. *Reading Black, Reading Feminist: A Critical Anthology*. New York: Meridian.

———. "Introduction: Darkly as through a Veil." In *The Souls of Black Folks* (1903), vii–xxix. New York: Bantam Books.

———. 1988. *The Signifying Monkey*. New York: Oxford University Press.

———. 1987. *Figures in Black*. Oxford: Oxford University Press.

Gever, Martha, John Greyson, and Pritibha Parmar, eds. 1993. *Queer Looks: Perspectives on Lesbian and Gay Film and Video*. London and New York: Routledge.

George, Nelson. 1994. *Blackface: Reflections on African-Americans and the Movies*. New York: HaperCollins Publishers.

————. 1992. *Buppies, B·Boys, Baps and Bohos: Notes on Post-Soul Black Culture.* Cambridge, MA: Da Capo.

Gilman, Sander L. *Disease and Representation: Images of Illness form Madness to AIDS.* Ithaca: Cornell University Press.

————. 1985. *Difference and Pathology: Stereotypes of Sexuality, Race and Madness.* Ithaca: Cornell University Press.

Gilroy, Paul. 1993. *The Black Atlantic: Modernity and Double Consciousness.* Cambridge, MA: Harvard University Press.

Glicksman, Marlaine. 1990. "They Gotta Have It." *Film Comment* (May-June).

Glover, David and Cora Kaplan. 2000. *Genders.* London and New York: Routledge.

Goffman, Erving. 1959. *The Presentation of the Self in Everyday Life.* New York: Doubleday.

Golden, Thelma, ed. 1994. *Black Men: Representations of Masculinity in Contemporary Art.* New York: Whitney Museum of American Art, Distributed by Harry N. Abrahams, Inc.

Gooding-Williams, Robert. 1995. "Black Cupids, White Desire: Reading the Representation of Racial Difference in *Casablanca* and *Ghost.*" In *Philosophy and Film,* edited by Cynthia Freeland and Thomas E. Wartenberg, 143–160. London and New York: Routledge.

Gordon, Lewis R. 2000. *Existentia Africana: Understanding Africana Existential Thought.* London and New York: Routledge.

————. 1997a. "Introduction." In *Existence in Black,* edited by Lewis Gordon, 1–9. London and New York: Routledge.

————. 1997b. "Existential Dynamics of Theorizing Blackness." In *Existence in Black,* edited by Gordon, 69–79. London and New York: Routledge.

————, ed. 1997c. *Existence in Black: An Anthology of Black Existential Philosophy.* London and New York: Routledge.

————. 1995a. *Bad Faith and Antiblack Racism.* Atlantic Highlands, NJ: Humanities Press.

————. 1995b. *Fanon and the Crisis of European Man: An Essay on Philosophy and the Human Sciences.* London and New York: Routledge.

Gray, Herman. 1995. *Watching Race: Television and the Struggle for "Blackness."* London and Minneapolis: University of Minnesota Press.

Green, J. Ronald. 1993. " 'Twoness' in the style of Oscar Micheaux." In *Black American Cinema,* edited by Manthia Diawara, 26–48. London and New York: Routledge.

Green, Ian. 1984. "Male Function." *Screen,* 25 (4): 36–48.

Guerrero, Ed. 1998. "A Circus of Dreams and Lies: The Black Film Wave at Middle Age." In *The New American Cinema,* edited Jon Lewis, 328–352. Durham and London: Duke University.

————. 1993. *Framing Blackness: The African American Image in Film.* Philadelphia: Temple University Press.

Guillory, Monique and Richard Green, editors. 1998. *Soul: Black Power, Politics, and Pleasure.* New York: New York University Press.

Gunning, Tom. 1991. *D. W. Griffith and the Origins of American Narrative Film.* Chicago: University of Chicago Press.

Hampton, Dream. 2000. "Soul Man." *Vibe* (April), 102–108.

Hanke, Robert. 1992. "Redesigning Men: Hegemonic Masculinity in Transition." In *Men, Masculinity, and the Media,* edited by Steve Craig, 185–199. London: Sage Publications.

———. 1990. "Hegemonic Masculinity in *thirtysomething.*" *Critical Studies in Mass Communication,* Volume 7: 231–248.

Harper, Phillip Brian. 1996. *Are We Not Men.* New York and Oxford: Oxford University Press.

———. 1994a. *Framing the Margins: The Social Logic of Postmodern Culture.* New York and Oxford: Oxford University.

———. 1994b. " 'The Subversive Edge': *Paris Is Burning,* Social Critique, and the Limits of Subjective Agency." *Diacritics,* 24 (2–3): 90–103.

Hearn, Jeff. 1998. "Theorizing men and men's theorizing." *Theory and Society,* Volume 27: 781–816.

Heywood, Ian. 1999. " 'Ever more specific': practices and perception in art and ethics." In *Interpreting Visual Culture,* edited by Ian Heywood and Barry Sandywell, 198–217. London and New York: Routledge.

Heywood, Ian and Barry Sandywell, eds. 1999. *Interpreting Visual Culture: Explorations in the Hermeneutics of the Visual.* London and New York: Routledge.

Hill, George H. and Sylvia Saverson Hill. 1985. *Blacks on Television: A Selectively Annotated Bibliography.* Metuchen, N. J. and London: The Scarecrow Press, Inc.

Holder, Geoffrey. 1986. *Adam.* New York: Viking Press.

Holland, Sharon Patricia. 2000. *Raising the Dead: Readings of Death and Black Subjectivity.* Durham and London: Duke University Press.

Holmlund, Christine Anne. 1993. "Displacing the Other" In *Otherness and the Media,* edited by Hamid Naficy and Teshome H. Gabriel, 1–22. New York: Harwood Academic Publishers.

hooks, bell. 1992. *Black Looks.* Boston: South End Press.

———. 1990. *Yearning: Race, Gender and Cultural Politics.* Boston: South End Press.

———. 1989. *Talking Back.* Boston: South End Press.

———. 1984. *Feminist Theory: From Margin to Center.* Boston: South End Press.

Horton, Luci. 1973. "Battle among the beauties: New Black Actresses Vie for the Top Film Roles." *Ebony* (November), 146–180.

Hoy, David Couzens and Thomas McCarthy. 1994. *Critical Theory.* Oxford and Cambridge, MA: Blackwell.

Hunter, Ian. 1988a. *Culture and Government.* New York and London: Routledge.

———. 1988b. "The Occasion of Criticism." *Poetics* 17.1–2: 159–84.

Hunter, Tera. 1989. "'It's a Man's Man's World': Specters of the Old Re-Newed in Afro-American Culture and Criticism." *Callaloo* 12 (1): 247–249.

Husserl, Edmund.1965. *Ideas: General Introduction to Pure Phenomenology.* Translated by W.R.Boyce Gibson. New York: Collier Books.

Hyatt, Marshall, ed. 1983. *The Afro-American Cinematic Experience: An Annotated Bibliography & Filmography.* Wilmington, Delaware: Scholarly Resources, Inc.

Jacobs, Ronald N. 2000. *Race, Media, and the Crisis of Civil Media: From Watts to Rodney King.* Cambridge and New York: Cambridge University Press.

Johnson, Albert. 1965. "The Negro in American Films: Some Recent Works." *Film Quarterly* (Summer): 14–30.

———. 1959. "Beige, Brown, or Black." *Film Quarterly* (Fall): 38–43.

Jones, Jacqui. 1991. "The New Ghetto Aesthetic." *Wide Angle,* 13 (3–4): 32–43.

Jones, LeRoi (Amiri Baraka). 1966. *Home.* New York: Morrow Paperback Editions.

Joyrich, Lynne. 1990. "Critical and Textual Hypermasculinity." In *Logics of Television,* ed. by Patricia Mellencamp, 156–172. Bloomington and Indianapolis: Indiana University Press.

Kant, Immanuel. 1798 (1978). *Anthropology from a Pragmatic Point of View.* Translated by Victor Lyle Dowell. Carbondale and Edwardsville: Southern Illinois University Press.

———. 1797 (1996). *The Metaphysics of Morals.* Translated by Mary Gregor. Cambridge and New York: Cambridge University Press.

———. 1785(1988). *Fundamental Principles of the Metaphysics of Morals.* Translated by T.K. Abbott. Buffalo, NY: Prometheus Books.

———. 1764 (1960). *Observations on the Feeling of the Beautiful and the Sublime.* Translated by John T. Goldthwait. Berkeley: University of California Press.

Kearny, Richard and Mark Dooley, editors. 1999. *Questioning Ethics: Contemporary Debates in Philosophy.* London and New York: Routledge.

Kelley, Robin D.G. 1997. *Yo Mama's Disfunktional: Fighting the Culture Wars.* Boston: Beacon Press.

———. 1994. *Race Rebels: Culture, Politics, and the Black Working Class.* New York: The Free Press.

Kellner, Douglas. 1995. *Media Culture.* London and New York: Routledge.

Kennedy, Lisa. 1990. "Wack House." *Village Voice,* March 13, 1990.

Kester, Gunilla Theander. 1995. *Writing the Subject: Bildung and the African American Text.* New York: Peter Lang.

King, Barry. 1991. "Articulating Stardom." In *Star Texts: Image and Performance in Film and Television,* edited by Jeremy G. Butler, 125–154. Detroit: Wayne State University Press.

Kristeva, Julia. 1982. *Powers of Horror: An Essay on Abjection.* Translated Leon S. Roudiez. New York: Columbia University Press.

Kupfer, Joseph H. 1999. *Visions of Virtue in Popular Film.* Boulder, Colorado: Westview Press.

Kymlicka, Will. 1991. "The Social Contract Tradition." In *A Companion to Ethics,* edited by Peter Singer, 186–196. Oxford: Blackwell Publishers.

Le Gouès, Thierry. 1997. *Soul: Photographs by Thierry Le Gouès.* Nates, France: Le Book Edition.

Leddick, David. 2000. *The Male Nude.* London and New York: Taschen.

Lee, Spike. 1991. *Five by Five: The Films of Spike Lee.* Edited by Shirley L. Poole. New York: Stewart, Tabori & Chang, Inc.

———. 1988. *Uplift the Race: The Construction of School Daze.* New York: Simon & Schuster.

Lehman, Peter. 1993. *Running Scared.* Philadelphia: Temple University Press.

Lehman, Peter, ed. 2001. *Masculinity: Bodies, Movies, Culture.* Routledge: London and New York.

Lejeune, Philippe. 1989. *On Autobiography.* Minneapolis: University of Minnesota Press.

Lentricchia, Frank and Thomas McLaughlin, editors. 1990. *Critical Terms of Literary Studies.* Chicago and London: University of Chicago Press.

Locke, Alain. 1989. *The Philosophy of Alain Locke.* Edited by Leonard Harris. Philadelphia: Temple University Press.

———. 1925a. "The New Negro." In *The New Negro,* edited by Locke, 3–16. New York: Macmillan Publishing Company.

———, ed. 1925b. *The New Negro.* New York: Macmillan Publishing Company.

Lott, Eric. 1994. "Cornel West in the Hour of Chaos: Culture and Race in *Race Matters.*" *Social Text,* 41 (Fall), 39–50.

Lott, Tommy. 1999. *The Invention of Race: Black Culture and the Politics of Representation.* Oxford: Blackwell Publishers.

———. 1991. "A No-Theory of Contemporary Black Cinema." *Black Literature Forum* 25 (Summer): 222–52.

McClintock, Anne. 1995. *Imperial Leather: Race, Gender, and Sexuality in the Colonial Contest.* London and New York: Routledge.

Madison, Gary Brent. 1981. *The Phenomenology of Merleau-Ponty.* Translated by the author. Athens, OH: Ohio University Press, reprinted in 1990.

Majors, Richard and Janet Mancini Billson. 1992. *Cool Pose: The Dilemma of Black Manhood in America.* New York: Simon & Schuster.

Mancini, Janet. 1980. *Strategic Styles: Coping in the Inner City.* Hanover, New Hampshire and London: University Press of New England.

Mandell, Richard D. 1984. *Sport: A Cultural History.* New York: Columbia University Press.

Mapplethorpe, Robert. 1988. *The Perfect Moment.* Philadelphia: Institute of Contemporary Art, University of Pennsylvania.

———. 1986. *Black Book.* New York: St. Martin's Press.

Marshall, P. David. 1997. *Celebrity and Power.* Minneapolis and London: University of Minnesota Press.

Mason, J. B. 1972. "New Films: Culture or Con Game." *Ebony Magazine* (December): 60–68.

May, Todd. 1995. *The Moral Theory of Postructuralism.* University Park, PA: Pennsylvania State University Press.

Maynard, Richard A. 1974. *The Black Man on Film: Racial Stereotyping.* Rochelle Park, New Jersey: Hayden Book Company, Inc.

Mayne, Judith. 1991. "A Parallax View of Lesbian Authorship." In *Inside/Out,* ed. by Diana Fuss, 173–184. New York and London: Routledge.

Mellencamp, Patricia, editor. 1990. *Logics of Television: Essays in Cultural Criticism.* Bloomington and Indianapolis: Indiana University Press.

Mercer, Kobena. 1994. *Welcome to the Jungle: New Positions in Black Cultural Studies.* London and New York: Routledge.

Merleau-Ponty, Maurice. 1964. *Sense and Nonsense.* Translated by Hubert L. Dreyfus and Patricia Allen Dreyfus. Evanston: Northwestern University Press.

———. 1962. *Phenomenology of Perception.* Translated by Colin Smith. London: Routledge, reprinted in 1994.

Messner, Michael A. 1997. *Politics of Masculinities: Men in Movements.* London: Sage Publications.

Miller, Toby. 1993. *The Well-Tempered Self: Citizenship, Culture, and the Postmodern Subject.* Baltimore: Johns Hopkins University Press.

Mills, Charles W. 1998. *Blackness Visible: Essays on Philosophy and Race.* Ithaca and London: Cornell University Press.

———. 1997. *The Racial Contract.* Ithaca and London: Cornell University Press.

Mirzoeff, Nicholas. 1999. *An Introduction to Visual Culture.* London and New York: Routledge.

———. 1998a. "What is visual culture?" In *The Visual Culture Reader,* edited by Mirzoeff, 3–13. London and New York: Routledge.

———, ed. 1998b. *The Visual Culture Reader.* London and New York: Routledge.

Morris, Pam, editor. 1984. *The Bakhtin Reader.* New York: Edward Arnold.

Morrison, Toni. 1992. *Playing in the Dark: Whiteness and the Literary Imagination.* Cambridge, MA: Harvard University Press.

Mosse, George L. 1985. *Nationalism and Sexuality: Middle-Class Morality and Sexual Norms in Modern Europe.* Madison: Wisconsin University Press.

Mostern, Kenneth. 1996. "Three Theories of the Race of W.E.B.DuBois." *Cultural Critique,* Fall: 27–63.

Moynihan, Daniel Patrick. 1965. "The Moynihan Report" [*The Negro Family Case for National Action*]. Washington, DC: US Department of Labor.

Mulvey, Laura. 1989. *Visual and Other Pleasures.* Bloomington and Indianapolis: Indiana University Press.

Murray, Albert. 1996. *The Blue Devils of Nada.* New York: Random House.

Naficy, Hamid and Teshome H. Gabriel, eds. 1993. *Otherness and the Media.* New York: Hardwood Academic Publishers.

Naremore, James. 1988. *Acting in the Cinema.* Berkeley: University of California Press.

Nathanson, Maurice, ed. 1973. *Phenomenology and the Social Sciences, Volume 1.* Evanston: Northwestern University Press.

Neal, Larry. 1989. *Visions of a Liberated Future.* Edited by Michael Schwartz. New York: Thunder's Mouth Press.

Neale, Steve. 1983. "Masculinity as Spectacle." *Screen,* Volume 24 (6): 2–16.

Newton, Ester. 1975. *Mother Camp: Female Impersonators in America.* Chicago: University of Chicago Press.

Olney, James. 1993. "The Value of Autobiography for Comparative Studies: African *vs* Western." In *African-American Autobiography,* ed. by William Andrews, 212–334. Englewood, New Jersey: Prentice Hall.

Omi, Michael and Howard Winant. 1994. *Racial Formations in the United States from the 1960's to the 1990's, 2nd Edition.* London and New York: Routledge.

Outlaw, Lucius T., Jr. 1996. *On Race and Philosophy.* London and New York: Routledge.

Paquet, Sandra Pouchet. 1993. "West Indian Autobiography." In *African-American Autobiography: A Collection of Critical Essays,* edited by William Andrews, 196–211. Englewood Cliffs, New Jersey: Prentice Hall.

Palmer, Richard E. 1969. *Hermeneutics: Interpretation Theory in Schleirmacher, Dilthey, Heidegger, and Gadamer.* Evanston, IL: Northwestern University Press.

Perkins, William Eric. 1996a. "The Rap Attack: An Introduction." In *Droppin' Science: Critical Essays on Rap Music and Hip Hop Culture,* ed. By William E. Perkins, 1–45. Philadelphia, PA: Temple University Press.

———, ed. 1996b. *Droppin' Science: Critical Essays on Rap Music and Hip Hop Culture.* Philadelphia, PA: Temple University Press.

Pietz, William. 1988. "The Problem of the Fetish, IIIa." *Res* 16 (Autumn): 105–124.

———. 1987. "The Problem of the Fetish, II." *Res* 13(Spring): 23–46.

———. 1985. "The Problem of the Fetish, I." *Res* 9(Spring): 5–17.

Poitier, Sidney. 2000. *The Measure of a Man.* San Francisco: HaperCollins.

———. 1980. *This Life.* New York: Knopf.

Posnock, Ross. 1998. *Color & Culture: Black Writers and the Making of the Modern Intellectual.* Cambridge, MA and London: Harvard University Press.

Potter, Russell. 1995. *Spectacular Vernaculars: Hip-Hop and the Politics of Postmodernisms.* Albany: State University of New York Press.

Questlove. 2000. "?uestlove Interviews D'Angelo." Online. http: //www.okayplayer.com/dangelo/interview.html

Rampersad, Arnold. 1990. *The Art and Imagination of W.E.B.DuBois.* New York: Schocken.

Regester, Charlene. 1994. "Stepin' Fetchit: The Man, the Image, and the African American Press." *Film History,* 6: 502–521.

Reid, Mark. 1993. *Redefining Black Cinema.* Berkeley, CA: University California.

Reid-Pharr, Robert F. 1997. "Tearing the Goat's Flesh: Homosexuality, Abjection, and the Production of Late-Twentieth-Century Black Masculinity." In *Novel Gazing: Queer Readings in Fiction,* edited by Sedgwick, 353–376. Durham and London: Duke University Press.

Reiter, Rayna, ed. 1975. *Towards an Anthropology of Women.* New York: Monthly Review Press.

Ricoueur, Paul. 1999. "Memory and Forgetting." In *Questioning Ethics: Contemporary Debates in Philosophy,* edited by Richard Kearney and Mark Dooley, 5–11. London and New York: Routeledge.

Rocchio,Vincent F. 2000. *Reel Racism: Confronting Hollywood's Construction of Afro-American Culture.* Boulder, Colorado: Westview Press.

Rose, Tricia. 1994. *Black Noise: Rap Music and Black Culture in Contemporary.* Hanover and London: Wesleyan University Press.

Ross, Andrew. 1994. "The Gangsta and the Diva." In *Black Male: Representations of Masculinity in Contemporary America.* Edited by Thelma Goldman. 159–166. New York: Whitney Museum Of American Art.

Rubin, Gayle. 1975. "The Traffic in Women: Notes on the 'Political Economy' of Sex." In *Towards an Anthropology of Women,* edited by Rayna Reiter, 157–210. New York: Monthly Review Press.

Russell, Catherine. 1999. *Experimental Ethnography: The work of film in the age of video.* Durham and London: Duke University Press.

Rutherford, Jonathan. 1988. "Who's That Man?" In *Male Order: Unwrapping Masculinity,* edited by Rowena Chapman and Jonathan Rutherford, 21–67. London: Lawrence & Wishart.

Sartre, Jean-Paul. 1956. *Being and Nothingness.* Translated by Hazel E. Barnes. New York: Washington Square Press.

Sartwell, Crispin. 1998. *Act Like You Know: African-American Autobiography and White Identity.* Chicago: University of Chicago Press.

Sayre, Henry. 1990. "Performance." In *Critical Terms of Literary Studies,* edited by Frank Lentricchia and Thomas McLaughlin, 91–104. Chicago and London: University of Chicago Press.

Schaefer, Eric. 1999. *"Bold, Daring, Shocking and True!": A History of Exploitation Films, 1919–1959.* Durham, North Carolina: Duke University Press.

Sedgwick, Eve Kosofsky, ed. 1997. *Novel Gazing: Queer Readings in Fiction.* Durham and London: Duke University Press.

———. 1993. "Queer Performativity." *GLQ,* 1(1): 1–16.

———. 1990. *Epistemology of the Closet.* Berkeley and Los Angeles: University of California Press.

———. 1985. *Between Men: English Literature and Male Homosocial Desire.* New York: Columbia University Press.

Sell, Mike. 2001. "The Black Arts Movement: Performance, Neo-Orality, and the Destruction of the 'White Thing.'" In *African American Performance and Theater History,* edited by Harry J. Elam, Jr. and David Krasner, 56–80. New York and Oxford: Oxford University Press.

Shohat, Ella and Robert Stam. 1998. "Narrativizing Visual Culture: Towards a Polycentric Aesthetics." In *The Visual Culture Reader,* edited by Nicholas Mirzoeff, 27–49. London and New York: Routledge.

———. 1994. *Unthinking Eurocentrism: Multiculturalism ad the Media.* London and New York: Routledge.

Shuker, Roy. 2001. *Understanding Popular Music (Second Edition).* London and New York: Routledge.

Siebers, Tobin. 1988. *The Ethics of Criticism.* Ithaca, NY: Cornell University Press.

Silverman, Kaja. 1995. *Male Subjectivity at the Margins.* London and New York: Routledge.

Simon, Richard. 1998. "The Stigmatization of Blaxploitation." In *Soul: Black Power, Politics, and Pleasure,* ed. by Monique Guillory and Richard Green, 236–49. New York: New York University Press.

Singer, Peter, editor. 1991. *A Companion to Ethics.* Oxford: Blackwell Publishers.

Smith, Valerie. 1998. *Not just race, not just gender: Black Feminist Readings.* London and New York: Routledge.

———. 1997a. "Introduction." In *Representing Blackness,* edited by Valerie Smith, 1–11. New Brunswick, New Jersey: Rutgers University Press.

————, ed. 1997b. *Representing Blackness: Issues in Film and Video.* New Brunswick, New Jersey: Rutgers University Press.

Snead, James A. 1994. *White Screens/Black Images: Hollywood from the Dark Side.* Edited by Colin MacCabe and Cornel West. London and New York: Routledge.

————. 1990. "Repetition as a Figure of Black Culture." In *Out There: Marginalization and Contemporary Cultures,* eds. Russell Ferguson, Martha Gever, Trinh T. Minh-ha and Cornel West, 213–32. Cambridge, MA: MIT Press.

————. 1985. "Recoding Blackness: The Visual Rhetoric of Black Independent Film." *Whitney Museum of American Art: The New American Filmmakers Series.* Program 23: 1–2.

Sobchack, Vivian. 1992. *The Address of the Eye: A Phenomenology of Film.* Princeton: Princeton University Press.

Sollars, Werner. 1986. *Beyond Ethnicity.* New York: Oxford University Press.

Solomon-Godeau, Abigail. 1997. *Male Trouble: A Crisis in Representation.* London and New York: Thames and Hudson.

————. 1995. "Male Trouble." In *Constructing Masculinity,* edited by Maurice Berger, *et.al.,* 69–76. London and New York: Routledge.

Spengemann, William and L.R. Lundquist. 1965. "Autobiography and the American Myth." *American Quarterly,* 17: 501–19.

Spivak, Gayatri Chakravorty. 1990. *The Post-Colonial Critic: Interviews, Strategies, Dialogues.* Edited by Sarah Harasym. London and New York: Routledge.

Stam, Robert. 1992. *Reflexivity in Film and Literature: From Don Quixote to Jean-Luc Godard.* New York: Columbia University Press.

————. 1989. *Subversive Pleasures: Bakhtin, Cultural Criticism, and Film.* Baltimore and London: Johns Hopkins University Press.

Stam, Robert, Robert Burgoyne, and Sandy Flitterman-Lewis. 1992. *New Vocabularies in Film Semiotics: Structuralism, Post-Structuralism and Beyond.* London and New York: Routledge.

Stecopolus, Harry and Michael Ubel, eds. 1997. *Race and the Subject of Masculinities.* Durham, NC: Duke University Press.

Steptoe, Robert B. 1979 (1991). *From Behind the Veil: A Study of Afro-American Narrative* (Second Edition). Chicago and Urbana: University of Illinois Press.

Stoller, Ann Laura. 1995. *Race and the Education of Desire.* Durham: Duke University Press.

Stone, Albert E. 1993. "After *Black Boy* and *Dusk of Dawn*: Patterns in Recent Black Autobiography." In *African-American Autobiography: A Collection of Critical Essays,* edited by William Andrews, 171–195. Englewood, New Jersey: Prentice Hall.

————. 1982. "Collaboration in Contemporary American Autobiography." *Revue française d'ètudes americaines,* 14: 151–65.

Taylor, Clyde R. 1998. *The Mask of Art: Breaking the Aesthetic Contract—Film and Literature.* Bloomington and Indianapolis: Indiana University Press.

Thomas, Kendall. 1996. "'Ain't Nothing Like the Real Thing': Black Masculinity, Gay Sexuality and the Jargon of Authenticity." In *Representing Black Men,* edited by Blount and Cunningham, 55–69. London and New York: Routledge.

Toback, James. 1971. *Jim: the Author's Self-Centered Memoir on the Great Jim Brown.* Garden City, New York: Doubleday & Company, Inc.

Vasey, Craig. 1999. "Being and Race." *Paidaia Archives* (November 28). Online: http://www.bu.edu/wcp/Papers/soci/sociVase.htm

Wallace, Michelle. 1990. *Invisibility Blues: From Pop to Theory.* London and New York: Verso.

———. 1978 (1990). *Black Macho and the Myth of the Superwoman.* London and New York: Verso.

Watkins, S. Craig. 1998. *Representing: Hip Hop Culture and the Production of Black Cinema.* Chicago and London: The University of Chicago Press.

Waugh, Thomas. 1993. "The Third Body: Patterns in the Construction of the Subject in Gay Male Narrative Film." In *Queer Looks,* edited by Martha Gever, et.al., 141–160. London and New York: Routledge.

Weiss, Gail. 1999. *Body Images: Embodiment as Intercorporeality.* London and New York: Routledge.

West, Cornel. 1993a. *Race Matters.* Boston: Beacon Press.

———. 1993b. *Keeping Faith: Philosophy and Race in America.* London and New York: Routledge.

———. 1990. "The New Cultural Politics of Difference." In *Out There: Marginalization and Contemporary Cultures,* edited by Russell Ferguson, Martha Gever, Trinh T. Minh-ha, and Cornel West, 19–36. Cambridge and London: MIT Press.

———. 1989. *The American Evasion of Philosophy: A Genealogy of Morals.* Madison, WI: University of Wisconsin Press.

———. 1982. *Prophesy Deliverance.* Philadelphia: Westminster Press.

Wiegman, Robyn. 1995. *Anatomies of Race: Theorizing Race and Gender.* Durham and London: Duke University Press.

———. 1991. "Black Bodies/American Commodities." In *Unspeakable Images,* ed. By Lester D. Friedman, 308–328. Urbana and Chicago: University of Chicago Press.

Williams, Carla. 1995. "The erotic image is naked and dark." In *Picturing Us,* edited by Deborah Willis, 129–136. New York: The New Press.

Williams, Saul. "Like the rain to the dirt from vine to the wine from the alpha of creation." Liner notes to *Voodoo* (1999) by D'Angelo. London and New York: Virgin Records.

Willis, Deborah, editor. 1994. *Picturing Us: African American Identity in Photography.* New York: The New Press.

Yearwood, Gladstone L. 2000. *Black Film as a Signifying Practice: Cinema, Narration, and the African-American Aesthetic Tradition.* Trenton, NJ and Asmara, Eritrea: Africa World Press.

———. 1982a. "Towards a Theory of Black Cinema Aesthetic." In *Black Cinema Aesthetics,* edited by Yearwood, 67–82. Athens, OH: Ohio University Press.

———, ed. 1982b. *Black Cinema Aesthetics: Issues in Independent Black Filmmaking.* Athens, OH: Ohio University Press.

Young, Robert J.C. 1995. *Colonial Desire: Hybridity in Theory, Culture and Race.* London and New York: Routledge.

Yùdice, George. 1995. "What's a Straight White Man to Do?" In *Constructing Masculinity,* edited by Maurice Berger, *et.al.,* 267–283. London and New York: Routledge.

Zack, Naomi. 2000. "The Good Faith of the Invisible man." *Paideia Archives,* February 11: 6 of 6. Online: http://www.bu.edu/wcp/Papers/Cult/CultZack.htm.

———. 1997. "Race, Death, Identity and Good Faith." In *Existence in Black,* edited by Lewis R. Gordon, 99–109. London and New York: Routledge.

# Index